The *Active Reader*

Book 3

Linda Kita-Bradley

Grass Roots Press

Edmonton, Alberta, Canada
2011

The Active Reader – Book 3 © 2011 Grass Roots Press

The Active Reader – Book 3 is published by

Grass Roots Press
A division of Literacy Services of Canada Ltd.
www.grassrootsbooks.net

AUTHOR	Linda Kita-Bradley
PASSAGES	Contributing Writer: Joyce Cameron
EDITOR	Pat Campbell
DESIGN	Lara Minja
LAYOUT	Susan Hunter
PILOTERS	Toronto Public Library, Adult Literacy Program, Downsview Branch

ACKNOWLEDGEMENTS

We acknowledge the financial support of the Government of Canada through the Book Publishing Industry Development Program (BPIDP) for our publishing activities.

We acknowledge the support of the Alberta Foundation for the Arts for our publishing programs.

ISBN 978-1-926583-17-4

Printed in Canada

Contents

About this workbook   iv

PEOPLE: Champions of Hope

Unit 1: Terry Fox   **1**

Unit 2: Viola Desmond   **11**

RELATIONSHIPS: In the Workplace

Unit 3: Personal Harrassment   **21**

Unit 4: Getting Along   **31**

HEALTH: Prevention

Unit 5: Food Poisoning   **41**

Unit 6: Skin Cancer   **51**

ENVIRONMENT: Oil Spills

Unit 7: Deepwater   **61**

Unit 8: The Cleanup   **71**

HISTORY: Fighting for Rights

Unit 9: Workers' Rights   **81**

Unit 10: Father of Medicare   **91**

Answer Key   **101**

About this workbook

Welcome to Book 3 of *The Active Reader* series. This workbook aims to engage learners in the process of active reading by providing stimulating reading passages that help learners develop the skills and strategies to become fluent readers.

The workbook is organized around five themes: people, relationships, health and safety, the environment, and history. Each theme consists of two units that provide the following activities:

Pre-reading
Photos and discussion questions introduce the topic, activate learners' background knowledge, and provide a purpose for reading.

Main Reading Passage
Learners are encouraged to read a non-fiction passage with strategically placed "Stop and Think" questions. Sidebars explain vocabulary or provide additional information to enhance readers' understanding.

Post-reading
Questions require students to recall factual information, make inferences, identify main idea, and make personal connections to the text.

Mini-Lesson
Learners focus on making inferences, finding main ideas, distinguishing between fact and opinion, and recognizing the organization of text.

Literacy Practice
Learners are encouraged to engage in daily literacy practices through reading, analyzing, and discussing text such as graphs, want ads, surveys, tables, maps, and cartoons.

Vocabulary
Learners gain a deep understanding of a theme-related word through activities that focus on the meaning of the target word as well as application of the word in different contexts.

Word Attack
Learners predict words in the context of a short paragraph as well as attending to letter patterns and the structure of words.

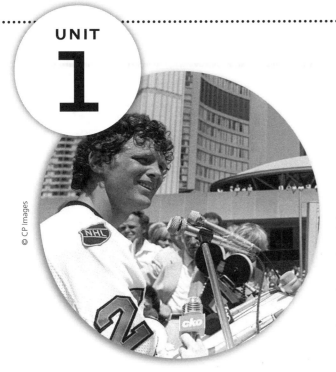

People
Terry Fox

Vocabulary: activism

Mini-Lesson: Making Inferences

Literacy Practice: Map

Terry Fox.

▶▶ Discussion

What do the words *power of hope* mean to you? Do you believe in the power of hope?

Terry Fox was born in Winnipeg, Manitoba, in 1958. He grew up in British Columbia. Terry lost his leg to bone cancer. Yet he gave hope to many people.

Read the passage on the next two pages. Learn how Terry gave hope to others.

Terry Fox

Terry Fox loved playing basketball. He wanted to play on the school team. The basketball coach told Terry to train as a runner. Instead, Terry spent every spare moment practising basketball. By Grade 10, Terry was captain of the basketball team.

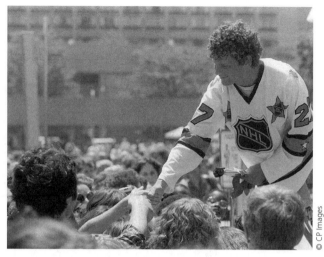

Terry gives hope to many people.

Stop and Think:

What does this paragraph tell you about Terry's character?

At age 18, Terry got shocking news. A pain in Terry's knee turned out to be bone cancer. Doctors had to remove Terry's right leg. Terry went through 16 months of treatment. In this time, he got to know other cancer patients. Some patients fought cancer with courage. Others lost hope. Many died.

Terry believed in the power of hope. He also believed more cancer research would give patients hope. Terry had read a story about a man who lost his leg to cancer. This man ran a marathon. The man inspired Terry. Terry started to plan a Marathon of Hope. The marathon would raise money for cancer research.

inspire: cause a person to feel they want to do something good.

On April 12, 1980, Terry stood on a rocky shore near St. John's, Newfoundland. It was Day 1 of the Marathon of Hope. Terry had trained for three years. He was ready to run across Canada. Only a few people came to cheer him on. Terry ran 17 cold kilometres that first day.

Stop and Think:

Imagine you are Terry. How do you feel as you start the Marathon of Hope? Explain why.

Slowly, people began to hear about the young man with one leg. They watched him run toward the West Coast. They watched him fight storms, heat, pain, and dizzy spells. They heard about his cause. They gave money to cancer research. Ten thousand people cheered Terry in downtown Toronto.

By Day 143, Terry had run over 5,000 kilometres. But just outside Thunder Bay, Ontario, Terry had to stop running. Cancer had spread to his lungs. As Terry fought for his life, the money poured in. Ten months later, Terry died at the age of 22.

The hope Terry gave to so many people lives on.

The Marathon of Hope raised over $27 million.

Terry's picture is on the back of Canada's 2005 loony.

▶▶ Check the Facts

1. Name three events that led to Terry running a Marathon of Hope. Check the passage to find the answer.

2. What is the most important idea in the passage?

(a) Terry Fox died from bone cancer.

(b) Terry Fox gave hope to people who had cancer.

▶▶ Discussion

1. Why do you think Terry Fox is a national hero? Give a reason for your answer.

2. Terry was inspired by a story that he read. Think about a time you felt inspired. Describe how and why you were inspired.

3. Each year, communities across Canada hold a Terry Fox Run. People can run or walk in this event. How can you find out if your community holds a Terry Fox Run? Would you take part in the run? Why or why not?

Mini-Lesson: Making Inferences

Look at the photo. What are these people getting ready to do?

© BigStockPhoto/Sandra Dunlap

Did you guess that they are getting ready to run a race? How did you know?

(1) You have a picture in your mind of what a race looks like. Your picture comes from what you know about runners and racing.

(2) The photo has clues that show the people are going to run a race. They are lined up. They are wearing running shorts and runners.

People often make guesses about what they see. These guesses are called inferences. People also make inferences when they read.

**Read the paragraph in the box.
What is the person's job?**

Did you say a nurse? Good for you. You have just made an inference. What did you already know about nurses? Which clues in the text helped you make the inference?

I do heavy work like lifting people. I take blood pressure. I take people's temperature. I work in a clinic or hospital.

Writers do not always tell us everything. So active readers make inferences as they read.

Read the sentences. Make inferences.
Explain why you made each inference.

What I saw	My inference	Why I made my inference
A dog was barking under a tree.	I think there was a cat in the tree.	Because I know that dogs often bark at cats.
1. A young boy blew out candles on a cake.	I think	
2. A woman was banging on a vending machine.	I think	

Now read the sentences about Terry Fox.
Make an inference.
Explain why you made the inference.

What I read	My inference	Why I made my inference
1. As he ran, Terry fought storms, heat, pain, and dizzy spells.	I think	Because I know that
2. Terry's picture is on the back of Canada's 2005 loony.	I think	Because I know that

5

Literacy Practice: Map

Maps provide a lot of information. They show where places are. They show borders between countries and provinces. Maps also show direction and distance.

Maps have many parts. They have a title, a key, a compass, and a scale.

© BigStockPhoto/Arunas Gabalis

Look at the map on the next page. Answer these questions:

Title

1. What is the title? Copy it here: _____

Key

The key explains the symbols on a map. For example, the symbol —— means a boundary between two countries.

2. How many symbols are in the map's key? _____

3. What does this symbol ★ tell us about a city?

   _____

4. Find the province of Ontario on the map. Find the city of Ottawa. The House of Commons is in Ottawa. Give a reason why.

   _____

Compass

A compass shows direction.

5. Find Thunder Bay on the map. Now circle the correct direction in this sentence:

   Thunder Bay is (south / west / east) of Ottawa.

Scale

A scale shows distance. The scale for this map shows 1,000 kilometres.

6. What is the distance between Toronto and St. John's?

   About (a) 1,000 kilometres (b) 2,000 kilometres (c) 3,000 kilometres

   How did you figure out your answer?

7. Find the capital city for your province or territory. About how far is

   the capital city from Ottawa? _____

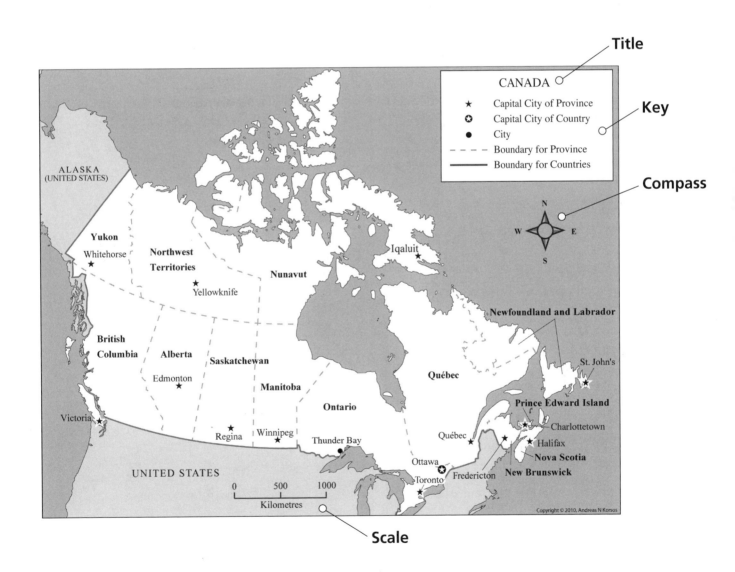

UNIT 1 • Terry Fox

Vocabulary

What do you mean when you say, "I know this word"? Knowing a word means many things. It means knowing how to say and spell the word. It means being able to explain and use the word.

Read this sentence: Terry Fox was an *activist*.

The activities below help you understand the word *activist*. Follow the directions in each box.

activist

1

An *activist* is a person who fights for something they believe in. An activist works hard to change society.

Read each question below. Circle the correct answer.

1. Which group of people did Terry Fox work hard for?

    (a) people who run marathons

    (b) people who have cancer

2. What important change did Terry bring to society?

    (a) There is more money for cancer research.

    (b) More people run marathons.

3. Why can we say that Terry Fox was an activist?

2

1. **Read about Scott, Joy, and Dell. Who is the activist? Explain your choice.**

    (a) Scott gave $2,000 to a home for pregnant teens.

    (b) Joy started a group. The group raises money. They build shelters for homeless teens.

    (c) Dell talked to his teenage son about safe sex.

2. **Do you know of any activists in your community? If yes,**

    (a) What change do they want to bring to society?

    (b) How are they trying to bring about this change?

Word Attack 1: Predict the Word

Finish the sentences in the paragraph.
You can use any words that make sense.

Maps provide a lot of information. Maps show

distance between two _____. The

distance is in miles or _____.

Maps also show us _____ such

as north and south. A _____ of

Canada shows territories and provinces.

> What do you do if you can't read a word?
>
> Active readers think of a word that makes sense.

Word Attack 2: Letter Patterns

Read the sentences.
Circle two words for each letter pattern.

ew

1. Terry grew up in British Columbia.
2. At age 18, Terry got very bad news.

ock

3. Terry got over the shocking news quickly.
4. Three years later, he stood on a rocky shore.

> Active readers look for letter patterns. A letter pattern looks and sounds the same. Say these words:
>
> **s**ound **r**ound **f**ound
>
> These words all have the same letter pattern.

ear

5. Terry began his marathon near St. John's.
6. People would soon hear about this brave young man.

Word Attack 3: Divide and Conquer

Read each sentence.
Circle the words that have a suffix.
The first one is an example.

1. Terry stood on a (rocky) shore.

2. He had trained for three years.

3. Few people cheered him on.

4. They watched Terry run through storms.

5. The money poured in.

Read the paragraph.
Add suffixes to complete the words.
The first one is an example.

At age 18, Terry got shock <u>ing</u> new_____. A

pain in his knee turn_____ out to be bone cancer.

Terry believe_____ in the power of hope. He

start_____ to plan a Marathon of Hope.

© CP Images

Read each sentence.
Find and divide the compound word.

1. The marathon started in Newfoundland.

2. People cheered in downtown Toronto.

3. The marathon ended outside Thunder Bay.

© Courtesy of the Office of
African Nova Scotian Affairs

People
Viola Desmond

Vocabulary: segregation

Mini-Lesson: Making Inferences

Literacy Practice: Cartoon

▶▶ Discussion

In the 1940s, many black people in Canada were poor. They still suffered from racism. White people could turn black people away from public places. Many black children could not attend school with white children.

Viola Desmond was born in Halifax, Nova Scotia, in 1914. Viola gave people hope that racism would end one day.

Read the passage on the next two pages. Learn how Viola gave people hope that racism would end.

© C.M.H.C./Library and Archives Canada/PA-170736

Black community in Halifax, 1958.

Equal Rights

In 1946, Viola took a business trip to the town of New Glasgow. In the evening, Viola went to see a movie. She did not know the theatre had a rule—black people had to sit in the balcony. The cashier refused to give Viola a main floor ticket. So, Viola paid for a balcony ticket. But she sat in a seat on the main floor. The manager asked Viola to move. She refused.

The police were called. They pulled Viola out of the theatre. After spending a night in jail, Viola went to court. She had no lawyer to defend her. The trial was short. She was found guilty. The charge? Tax evasion. The tax on a main floor ticket was two cents. But Viola had only paid the one-cent tax on the balcony ticket. The unpaid penny was used as an excuse to punish Viola.

tax evasion: not paying taxes that, by law, should be paid

Stop and Think:

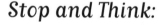

What was the real reason Viola was put in jail?

Viola had to pay a $20 fine or spend 30 nights in prison. Viola paid the fine. She asked the black community to help her fight the court's decision. The NSAACP raised money for a lawyer. A newspaper for black people picked up Viola's story. Then other newspapers started to report her case. Many people supported Viola. After two appeals, Viola won her case.

NSAACP: Nova Scotia Association for the Advancement of Coloured People

Nova Scotia's black community kept up the fight for equal rights. In 1954, the government of Nova Scotia passed new laws. Owners of public places had to serve black people. Separate schools for black children had to be shut down. These laws did not end racism. But they were a big step forward.

On April 14, 2010, the government of Nova Scotia gave Viola a free pardon. Some people were happy with the pardon. Other people were angry. "Why does Viola need a pardon?" they asked. "She did nothing wrong."

> A **free pardon** gives a person a clean criminal record.

Stop and Think:

**Imagine you are a member of Viola's family.
How do you feel about Viola's free pardon? Why?**

▶▶ Check the Facts

1. Explain how Viola's court case became famous.
   Check the passage to find the answer.

2. What is the most important idea in the passage?

   (a) Viola Desmond refused to sit in the balcony.

   (b) Viola Desmond helped change racist laws.

▶▶ Discussion

1. Why do you think the government finally gave Viola a pardon?

2. Describe a time when you stood up for something you believed in.
   What was the result? How did you feel?

3. Do you think racism continues to be a problem? Give a reason for
   your answer. How can (a) workplaces, (b) schools, and (c) parents
   fight racism?

Mini-Lesson: Making Inferences

The writer does not always tell readers everything.
So readers make inferences.

You can make an inference by using what you
already know and looking for clues in the text.

Read the sentences about Viola in the chart.
Make inferences.
Explain why you made each inference.

What I read	My inference	Why I made the inference
A business trip took Viola to the town of New Glasgow.	I think Viola had a good job.	Because I know that people with good jobs go on business trips.
1. The police pulled Viola out of the theatre.	I think	Because I know that
2. The trial was short. Viola was found guilty.	I think	Because I know that

Courtesy of the Office of African Nova Scotian Affairs

Read the paragraphs.
Make inferences.
Explain why you made each inference.

Paragraph 1

Viola wanted to work in a beauty salon. Beauty schools in Halifax turned Viola away because she was black. So Viola trained in Montreal and New York. She went back to Halifax. She opened her own beauty salon and school.

My inference:

I think _____

_____ .

Paragraph 2

Viola had a sister named Wanda. Wanda did not speak up as much as Viola. Wanda would get angry or complain to her friends. But she did little to right any wrongs that were done to her. Later in life, Wanda started to stick up for herself.

My inference:

I think _____

_____ .

Literacy Practice: Cartoon

Cartoons make people laugh—or at least smile. Cartoons also make people think about important topics.

A cartoon has two main parts: a drawing
                                   a caption

The caption helps you understand the cartoon. The caption tells you what a character is saying. Sometimes the caption describes what is happening in the cartoon.

Look at the cartoon on page 17.
It shows a boss and an employee named Dan.
Answer these questions:

1. Read the caption.
   Who is saying these words? (a) Dan   (b) the boss

2. (a) Do you think the boss is treating Dan as an equal?
       What, in the drawing, helped you get your answer?

   (b) Describe how the boss is treating Dan.

3. (a) Look at Dan. How do you think he feels?

   (b) How would you feel in Dan's place? Why?

4. What is the main message of the cartoon?
   Circle the correct answer.

   (a) Adult men do not like to sit in children's rocking chairs.

   (b) Some people's words do not match their actions.

   (c) Bosses do not like their employees.

"Now, Dan, we're all equals here. Have a seat." — Caption

Vocabulary

Read this sentence: Black people have been victims of *segregation*.

The activities below help you understand the word *segregation*. Follow the directions in each box.

(1) segregation **(2)**

1

Read the meaning of *segregation*:

segregation: the act of separating a group of people from society because of race, class, or religion

1. **Now read the words below. Tick two words that describe segregation.**

   _____ (a) divide

   _____ (b) include

   _____ (c) apart

2. **In the past, black children had to go to black schools. Explain why this is an example of segregation.**

2

Read the examples below. Choose the example that describes an act of segregation. Explain your choice.

(a) The police put Viola Desmond in jail. Viola stayed in jail for one night.

(b) Greek people in a community chose to set up a Greek school for their children.

(c) In 1939, the German Nazis moved Jewish people to ghettos.

Word Attack 1: Predict the Word

Finish the sentences in the paragraph.
You can use any words that make sense.

Many people enjoy cartoons. Cartoons make people

_____ . Cartoons talk about

_____ topics. Cartoons give people

a chance to express their _____ .

Cartoons make people feel _____ .

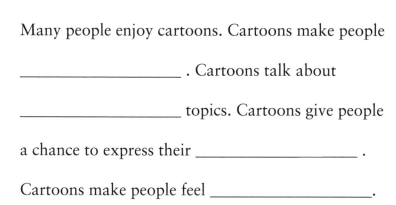

What do you do if you can't read a word?

Active readers think of a word that makes sense.

Word Attack 2: Letter Patterns

Read the sentences.
Circle two words for each letter pattern.

ace

1. Every public place had to serve all people.
2. Owners had to serve people of all races.

ight

3. Viola spent a long night in jail.
4. The black community helped Viola fight racism.

uilt

5. The lawyers built a case against the theatre.
6. Why did Viola get a pardon? She was not guilty to start with.

Active readers look for letter patterns. A letter pattern looks and sounds the same. Say these words:

sound **r**ound **f**ound

These words all have the same letter pattern.

Word Attack 3: Divide and Conquer

Read each sentence.
Circle the words that have a suffix.
The first one is an example.

1. Viola (asked) for a ticket to see a movie.

2. She wanted a ticket for the main floor.

3. The police pulled Viola out of the theatre.

4. After spending a night in jail, Viola went to court.

5. After two appeals, Viola won her case.

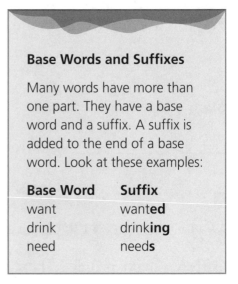

Base Words and Suffixes

Many words have more than one part. They have a base word and a suffix. A suffix is added to the end of a base word. Look at these examples:

Base Word	Suffix
want	want**ed**
drink	drink**ing**
need	need**s**

Read the paragraph.
Add suffixes to complete the words.
The first one is an example.

In 1954, the government of Nova Scotia pass _ed___

new laws. Own_____ of public place_____ had to

serve black people. Separate school_____ for black

children had to be shut down. These law_____ did

not end racism. But they help_____ fight racism.

© Bettman/Corbis

Read each sentence.
Find and divide the compound word.

1. Many newspapers picked up Viola's story.

2. Everyone knew about her case.

3. Do you agree that Viola did nothing wrong?

Compound Words

Compound words are made from two or more little words.

butterfly   butter / fly

Relationships

Personal Harassment

Vocabulary: exploit

Mini-Lesson: Main Idea and Details

Literacy Practice: Want Ad

▶▶ Discussion

Think about your favourite job.
What did you like about it?

Think about your worst job.
What did you dislike about it?

Read the passage on the next two pages.
Learn why Flo is not happy in her job.

Personal Harassment

Flo cooks in a fishing camp. One day, the boss gave Flo a pot. "Cook this up for me," he said. Flo looked in the pot and screamed. A snake lay curled up inside. Flo walked away in anger. She was tired of her boss's practical jokes. "Hey! Where's your sense of humour?" the boss asked.

Flo's boss thinks he is being funny. But he's not. He is harassing Flo. In some cases, personal harassment is clear. It can include repeated insults, threats, mean behaviour, and unwanted touching. And, as in Flo's case, it can include repeated practical jokes.

Stop and Think:

When do you think practical jokes turn into harassment? Read on. Are your ideas in the passage?

> Personal harassment is against the law.

At times, harassment is not so clear. Let's say a boss treats workers like children; he talks down to them. Being treated like a child makes people feel small. And being talked down to makes people angry. But how can a person tell when behaviour is harassment?

The answer can lie in the victim's feelings and actions. Does the victim no longer feel welcome at work? Does the victim start to take sick days just to avoid the harasser? Is the victim's work suffering? Personal harassment makes a person feel bad. It affects how a person does their work.

Stop and Think:

Imagine your boss is harassing you at work. Why might your work suffer?

Many victims of harassment ignore what is going on. They fear they will lose their job if they act to stop the harassment.

But turning a blind eye does not usually help. If the victim feels safe, they can ask the harasser to stop. The victim should be polite and clear, but firm. The victim may want someone with them as a witness.

If the harassment does not stop, the victim should jot down notes. The notes should include the dates of the harassment, who was there, and what was said or done. This information will help the CHRC help the victim of harassment.

No one should have to suffer harassment in silence.

> **CHRC**: (Canadian Human Rights Commission) This group helps people who may be victims of harassment. You can find their toll-free number online.

. . . .

▶▶ Check the Facts

1. Find three ways that people deal with harassment. Check the passage to find the answer.

2. What is the most important idea in the passage?
(a) Learn how to spot personal harassment. Then deal with it.
(b) Personal harassment makes people's work suffer.

▶▶ Discussion

1. Are the following examples harassment? Explain why or why not.
(a) The boss always scolds you for being late.
(b) The boss ignores you, except when he wants to make fun of you.
(c) The boss loses his temper one day and calls you an idiot.

2. Imagine you are harassed at work. Do you deal with the harassment? Or do you suffer in silence? Give a reason for your behaviour.

3. Some people feel they have the power to harass others. For example, a boss might harass workers just because he is the boss. Why else do some people harass others?

Mini-Lesson: Main Idea and Details

A paragraph has two parts: (1) a main idea and

                              (2) supporting details

The main idea is the important idea. The details support the main idea.
The details help the reader understand the main idea. Active readers
look for main ideas and supporting details.

How do I find the main idea of a paragraph?

Ask yourself the following question:
What does the writer want me to learn from this paragraph?

How do I know I have found the main idea?

Find two or three details that support the main idea. If you can find
supporting details, you know you have found the main idea.

**Read the paragraph below.
The main idea is underlined.**

Sara was a welder. <u>One co-worker always
harassed Sara.</u> He called Sara names like "Butch."
He hid Sara's tools all the time. Sara tried to
ignore him. She ended up quitting.

**Now find two supporting details for the main idea.
Write the details on the lines.**

1. _____

2. _____

RELATIONSHIPS

Read each paragraph.
Choose the correct main idea from the box.
Find supporting details in the paragraph. Write them on the lines.

Paragraph 1

Many victims of harassment ignore what is going on. They fear they will lose their job if they act to stop the harassment. But, turning a blind eye does not usually help. If the victim feels safe, they can ask the harasser to stop. The victim should be polite and clear, but firm. The victim may want someone with them as a witness.

(a) People lose their jobs sometimes.

(b) A witness is never harassed.

(c) There are different ways to deal with harassment.

Supporting details:

1. _____

2. _____

Paragraph 2

If the harassment does not stop, the victim should jot down notes. The notes should include the dates of the harassment, who was there, and what was said or done. This information will help the CHRC help the victim of harassment.

(a) The notes should include the dates of the harassment.

(b) The victim should jot down notes about the harassment.

(c) CHRC means Canadian Human Rights Commission.

Supporting details:

1. _____

2. _____

3. _____

Literacy Practice: Want Ad

Finding a job is a skill. People find jobs in different ways. One way to find a job is to ask family and friends for leads. Another way is to search the want ads. Want ads appear in newspapers and online.

Think about want ads you have seen. Discuss these questions:

1. What information would you expect to see in a want ad? Add your ideas to the list below:

   employer's contact information

   _____   _____

   _____   _____

2. Want ads use a lot of short forms. Look at the bolded short forms below. What do you think they mean? Write your ideas.

   (a) $12.50/**hr** _____   (d) Diploma **req'd** _____

   (b) 40 **hrs/wk** _____   (e) **F/T** shift work _____

   (c) No **exp** needed _____   (f) **P/T** shift work _____

Check your ideas for questions 1 and 2 in the Answer Key.

Now read Want Ads 1 and 2 on the next page.
Both ads are for a Food Service Manager.
Compare the two ads by filling in the chart.

Want Ad 1

Food Service Manager.
The Coffee Hut. P/T leading to F/T.
Shift work. $12.62/hr + benefits.
Exp not needed. Will train. Apply in
person or by email: abc@mail.ca

Want Ad 2

Food Service Manager req'd.
Happy Day Cafe. F/T $15/hr,
40 hrs/wk (shift) Manage staff
and work schedule. Keep record of
stock. Five years exp req'd. Need
computer skills. Send resumé by
email: xyz@mail.com

Want Ad 1: The Coffee Hut	Want Ad 2: Happy Day Cafe
List 2 reasons you would apply.	List 2 reasons you would apply.
List 2 reasons you would not apply.	List 2 reasons you would not apply.

Which job would you apply for? Why?
How would you like to apply for a job? By email or in person? Explain why.
What other information would you like to know about the job?

Vocabulary

Read this sentence: The leader of the cleaning crew *exploits* the workers.

The activities below help you understand the word *exploit*.
Follow the directions in each box.

exploit

1

Read the meaning of *exploit*:

> **exploit:** use someone or something unfairly for your own benefit

**Read about Sherry and Rex.
Sherry is exploiting Rex.**

> Sherry is the leader of a cleaning crew. Rex is new to the crew. He really needs the work. Sherry makes Rex do all the dirty jobs. She makes Rex do all the paperwork at the end of the day.

Answer these questions:

1. How is Sherry exploiting Rex?
2. What benefit is Sherry getting?
3. Rex does not complain. Why not?

2

**Read about May and Leo.
Answer the questions.**

1. May is a newcomer to Canada. She does not have a work visa. The boss makes May work overtime with no extra pay.

   (a) The boss is exploiting May. What benefit is he getting?

   (b) May does not complain. Why not?

2. Leo needs more money. So he works as a barber part-time. Leo has a friend named Rick. Rick always asks Leo for free haircuts. He always asks Leo for free hair products.

   (a) Who is exploiting whom?

   (b) What benefit is he getting?

   (c) Why do you think Leo does not complain?

Word Attack 1: Predict the Word

Finish the sentences in the paragraph.
You can use any words that make sense.

Finding a job is not always easy. Looking at want ads

is a _____ way to find a job. You can

find want ads in _____ or online. Want

ads tell you about things like _____

and pay. You can send your _____ in

by fax or email.

> What do you do if you can't read a word?
>
> Active readers think of a word that makes sense.

Word Attack 2: Letter Patterns

Read the sentences.
Circle two words for each letter pattern.

oss

1. My boss plays a lot of practical jokes.

2. His jokes are his loss. We lose time on the job.

ick

3. My boss picks on me all the time.

4. I pretend to be sick so I can stay away from work.

> Active readers look for letter patterns. A letter pattern looks and sounds the same. Say these words:
>
> **s**ound **r**ound **f**ound
>
> These words all have the same letter pattern.

ould

5. A victim of harassment should bring a witness.

6. A harasser could get angry if you ask them to stop.

Word Attack 3: Divide and Conquer

Read each sentence.
Circle the words that have a suffix.
The first one is an example.

1. (Harassment) can include mean jokes.

2. It can include unwanted touching.

3. It includes repeated bad behaviour.

4. A boss treats workers like children.

5. Harassment makes people feel bad.

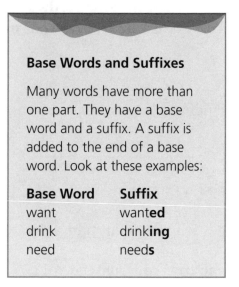

Base Words and Suffixes

Many words have more than one part. They have a base word and a suffix. A suffix is added to the end of a base word. Look at these examples:

Base Word	Suffix
want	want**ed**
drink	drink**ing**
need	need**s**

Read the paragraph.
Add suffixes to complete the words.
The first one is an example.

Many victim_s____ of harassment ignore what is

go_____ on. But turn_____ a blind eye does not

usually help. If the victim feel_____ safe, they can

ask the harasser to stop.

© BigStockPhoto/Lisa F. Young

Read each sentence.
Find and divide the compound word.

1. A workplace should be safe.

2. Bring someone as a witness.

3. She wants something from me.

Compound Words

Compound words are made from two or more little words.

butterfly   butter / fly

Relationships

Getting Along

Vocabulary: assertive

Mini-Lesson: Main Idea and Details

Literacy Practice: Survey

▶▶ **Discussion**

Nobody's perfect. At times, even people we like can drive us crazy—especially at work. Do you think it is important to get along with co-workers? Why or why not?

Read the passage on the next two pages. Learn how people can get along with their co-workers.

Getting Along

Do you want to keep your job and enjoy your work? Getting along with co-workers will help. But sometimes, even people we like can act in ways that make us feel uneasy. What can we do in these cases? We cannot change our co-workers. But we can change how we respond to their behaviour.

© BigStockPhoto/Robert Gebbie

Here are some ways to respond to unwanted behaviour in the workplace.

Stop and Think:

Give an example of unwanted behaviour in the workplace. Read on. Is your example in the passage?

Gossiping: Many co-workers think gossip is harmless. But gossip can hurt morale and end in distrust. A workplace becomes more pleasant when we try to stop gossip. We can speak well of the person who is a victim of gossip. Better yet, we can change the subject. Or we can say, "I like talking to you, but let's not talk about other people."

Complaining: Co-workers who complain need good listeners. Good listeners ask questions. Asking questions shows that we want to hear more. So we need to change how we listen. We need to stop asking questions. Instead, we can say, "I'm sorry you are having a bad day." Then we can change the subject. Or we can say nothing and let our silence give the hint.

Stop and Think:

What hint do you think we give by our silence?

Blaming: When things go wrong, some co-workers do not want to take responsibility. They worry about getting into trouble. So they blame others. When someone starts blaming, we can change the direction of the conversation. We can say, "Let's not worry about who did it. Let's just try to fix it."

Knowing-It-All: Some co-workers need to talk as if they know everything. This helps them feel good about themselves. There is no point in arguing with them. We can smile and say, "Your way sounds like it works for you. I like to do it another way."

We all want to get along with our co-workers. At times, it takes careful thinking to do this with skill.

....

▶▶ Check the Facts

1. One main way to respond to gossiping is to change the subject. Find one main way to respond to (a) complaining, (b) blaming, and (c) knowing-it-all. Check the passage to find the answers.

2. What is the most important idea in the passage?

(a) Learn how to respond to unwanted behaviour in co-workers.

(b) Try to change unwanted behaviour in co-workers.

▶▶ Discussion

1. Some people complain a lot. How do you think these people might affect (a) their co-workers and (b) the workplace?

2. Describe a time when you had to deal with unwanted behaviour. How did you feel about the results? Explain why.

3. Imagine a co-worker's unwanted behaviour does not change, no matter what you say or do. What are your possible next steps?

Mini-Lesson: Main Idea and Details

A paragraph has two parts. The main idea is the important idea. The details support the main idea. The details help the reader understand the main idea.

To find the main idea, ask yourself the following question:

What does the writer want me to learn from this paragraph?

If you find the main idea, you can also find supporting details.

Read each paragraph below.
Choose the correct main idea from the box.

Paragraph 1

A workplace becomes more pleasant when we try to stop gossip. We can speak well of the person who is a victim of gossip. Better yet, we can change the subject. Or we can say, "I like talking to you, but let's not talk about other people."

(a) It is helpful to talk to people that we like.

(b) There are different ways to stop gossip.

(c) Some workplaces are pleasant.

Now find three supporting details in the paragraph. Write the details on the lines.

1. _____

2. _____

3. _____

Paragraph 2

Co-workers who complain need good listeners. Good listeners ask questions. Asking questions shows that we want to hear more. So we need to change how we listen. We need to stop asking questions.

(a)	People who complain ask a lot of questions.
(b)	Some co-workers complain.
(c)	We need to change how we listen to people who complain.

Supporting details:

1. _____

2. _____

Paragraph 3

Even people we like can act in ways that make us feel uneasy. What can we do in these cases? We cannot change our co-workers. But we can change how we respond to their behaviour. At times, it takes careful thinking to do this with skill.

(a)	Co-workers have a lot of skills.
(b)	It is not easy to deal with unwanted behaviour.
(c)	Everybody needs to change their behaviour.

Supporting details:

1. _____

2. _____

3. _____

Literacy Practice: Survey

A survey is a list of questions or statements. People use surveys to get information.

Magazines often have surveys. You can take these surveys to learn about yourself. Surveys cover many topics. For example, a survey can tell you how well you get along with co-workers.

Some surveys are based on research. Other surveys are for fun.

Take the survey below.
Read each statement.
Put a number from 1 to 5 beside each statement.

The numbers mean:
1. Never   2. Rarely   3. Sometimes   4. Usually   5. Always

How assertive are you?

(Assertive means being confident enough to say or do what you want.)

1. I can say "no" to friends. _____

2. I can ask to be paid back for borrowed money. _____

3. I tell someone when I disagree with them. _____

4. I make decisions easily. _____

5. I return things to a store if I'm not happy with them. _____

6. I can say "no" to sales people. _____

7. If others criticize me, I do not get angry. _____

8. I speak up when someone treats me unfairly. _____

9. I can speak in front of groups. _____

10. I ask for help when I need it. _____

11. I can show love and affection. _____

12. I can make new friends. _____

13. I can accept compliments easily. _____

14. I tell co-workers when their actions bother me. _____

15. I can turn down an invite if I don't want to go. _____

16. I tell my landlord when my apartment needs repairs. _____

17. I can ask for time off at work when I need it. _____

Now add up your total score and write it here: _____

Source: adapted with permission from *Making It Work, Action Read.*

This is what your score means:

Less than 30: You are assertive only when you have no choice. You wish you could speak up more. Sometimes you feel angry with yourself when you do not speak up. Sometimes you feel that you let others push you around.

Between 31 and 45: You are assertive but only at certain times with certain people. For example, you can be assertive with people in your family. But you cannot be assertive with strangers.

Between 46 and 60: You are assertive. But there are still times when you are silent. For example, you might find it hard to tell a doctor you want a second opinion. Then later you wish you had spoken your mind.

Between 61 and 75: You are very assertive. You speak your mind in most situations. You do what you need to do to get things done.

Do you agree with what your score means?
Explain why or why not.

Vocabulary

Read this sentence: The *assertive* worker put a stop to the gossip.

The activities below help you understand the word *assertive*.
Follow the directions in each box.

assertive

1

Read the paragraphs below. As you read, try to figure out the meaning of *assertive*.

> Josh was tired of Fred's gossip. Josh decided to be *assertive*. "Listen Fred," said Josh, "Let's not talk about people." Fred didn't gossip around Josh anymore.

• • • • •

> A big man butted into a long lineup. An *assertive* woman said, "Excuse me, sir, but the end of the line is over there."

Now choose the correct meaning for assertive.

(a) confused

(b) acting in a way that hurts people

(c) sure enough of yourself to speak your mind; confident

2

Read about Shane. He has a problem.

> Shane worked late every day. But he could not catch up on his work. He started to worry and lose sleep. Then Shane's boss called him into the office. "I have a new big project for you," said the boss.

Shane decided to be assertive. What did he do? Circle the correct answer. Give a reason for your choice.

(a) He said, "Okay" and worked weekends.

(b) He said, "Okay, but I am too busy to start the project right now."

(c) He blew up and yelled, "I quit!"

Word Attack 1: Predict the Word

Finish the sentences in the paragraph.
You can use any words that make sense.

Surveys cover many topics. For example, a survey can

tell you how assertive you are. Or a survey can tell you

if you make _____ easily. A survey can

also tell you if you get along with _____.

Surveys are _____ to do.

> What do you do if you can't read a word?
>
> Active readers think of a word that makes sense.

Word Attack 2: Letter Patterns

Read the sentences.
Circle two words for each letter pattern.

ore

1. A workplace without gossip is more pleasant.
2. Listening to gossip can become a chore.

eed

3. People who complain need good listeners.
4. People who complain feed on questions.

> Active readers look for letter patterns. A letter pattern looks and sounds the same. Say these words:
>
> **s**ound **r**ound **f**ound
>
> These words all have the same letter pattern.

ong

5. When things go wrong, some people blame others.
6. Be strong. Don't join in the "blame game."

Word Attack 3: Divide and Conquer

Read each sentence.
Circle the words that have a suffix.
The first one is an example.

1. (Sometimes) things go wrong.

2. People are afraid of being fired.

3. They start pointing fingers at co-workers.

4. In this case, try fixing the problem.

5. Talking about a problem often helps.

Base Words and Suffixes

Many words have more than one part. They have a base word and a suffix. A suffix is added to the end of a base word. Look at these examples:

Base Word	Suffix
want	want**ed**
drink	drink**ing**
need	need**s**

Read the paragraph.
Add suffixes to complete the words.
The first one is an example.

There are many kind_s___ of unwant_____

behaviour such as complain_____ and gossip_____ .

We all want to get along with our co-worker_____ .

At time_____ , it take_____ careful think_____ to

do this with skill.

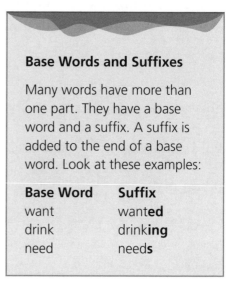

© BigStockPhoto/Lisa F. Young

Read each sentence.
Find and divide the compound word.

1. We cannot change our co-workers.

2. Change the subject when someone gossips.

3. Some people talk as if they know everything.

Compound Words

Compound words are made from two or more little words.

butterfly   butter / fly

© BigStockPhoto/Jim Lopes

Health
Food Poisoning

Vocabulary: cautious

Mini-Lesson: Fact and Opinion

Literacy Practice: Recipe

© BigStockPhoto/Caroline Klapper

▶▶ Discussion

Each year, up to 13 million people in Canada get food poisoning. There are many ways to prevent food poisoning. You can wash your hands before and after handling food. How else can you prevent food poisoning?

Food poisoning is easy to prevent. But sometimes, people do get sick.

Read the passage on the next two pages. Learn how Maya got food poisoning.

Food Poisoning

Maya took the leftover lunch meat out of the fridge. She checked the meat for green spots. She smelled the meat. It smelled okay. So Maya made a sandwich. The next day, Maya got a fever. Soon she had stomach cramps and was throwing up. Maya had food poisoning.

Bacteria are the leading cause of food poisoning. Bacteria grow in meat, fish, poultry, and dairy products. They grow best in warm, damp places. Maya learned that some bacteria do not cause food to smell or look bad. But these bacteria can still cause food poisoning. It is important to know how to handle food in order to cut down on bacteria.

© iStockphoto/Sumners Graphics Inc.

Shopping for food: Check food packages for rips and leaks. Read the expiry dates. Check uncooked food for freshness. Is the hamburger a healthy red colour or a stale grey? Buy fridge and freezer foods last.

Stop and Think:

Why do you think you should buy fridge and freezer foods last?

Storing food: Put food in the fridge or freezer within an hour after buying it. Cook meat, fish, and chicken within two days. Or put these foods in the freezer. After cooking, do not let food sit out for more than two hours. Keep all leftovers cold and use them within four days.

bacteria: small living cells that you can see only with a microscope

poultry: food such as chicken, turkey, duck, and goose

Preparing food: Thaw food in the fridge, not at room temperature. Or put food in a plastic bag. Then run cold water over the bag. Keep vegetables and milk products away from raw meat, poultry, and fish. For example, if you cut up chicken, wash the knife and cutting board in hot water and soap. Then cut up other food, like vegetables. Also, cook food properly. Note cooking times and temperatures.

Stop and Think:

How do you usually thaw food?

Like Maya, some people get very sick from food poisoning. If you get food poisoning, drink a lot of liquids. Avoid caffeine and sugar. See a doctor if symptoms last more than two days.

. . . .

▶▶ Check the Facts

1. Find three ways to cut down on bacteria when you prepare food. Check the passage to find the answer.

2. What is the most important idea in the passage?

(a) Bacteria can grow in hot food.

(b) It is important to know how to store, handle, and shop for food.

▶▶ Discussion

1. Let's say Maya uses tongs to put burger patties on a barbecue. Then Maya uses the tongs to serve salad. Why is Maya at risk of getting food poisoning?

2. What do you have in your fridge right now? When was the last time you checked expiry dates? How old are your leftovers?

3. The symptoms of stomach flu are similar to the symptoms of food poisoning. How would you know whether you had food poisoning or the flu? Would you visit a doctor? Why or why not?

Mini-Lesson: Fact and Opinion

Do you ever disagree with an idea? If so, you have an opinion. An opinion is a belief. It is a way of thinking about something. Sometimes an opinion is hard to prove.

Facts are different from opinions. Facts can be proven. A fact is 100 percent true.

Active readers know the difference between facts and opinions.

Look at each pair of sentences.
Write F beside the sentence that is a fact.
Write O beside the sentence that is an opinion.

1. _____ It is 21°C today.

   _____ It is too warm today.

2. _____ He did bad on the test.

   _____ He got 63 percent on the test.

3. _____ Baseball is played in Canada.

   _____ Everyone loves baseball.

4. _____ Canada is the best country.

   _____ Ottawa is the capital of Canada.

Look at the sentences.
Tick F for the sentences that are facts.
Tick O for the sentences that are opinions.

	F	O
1. Up to 13 million people in Canada get food poisoning each year.		
2. Bacteria grow in warm, damp places.		
3. Food poisoning is not serious.		
4. Ducks are an example of poultry.		
5. Hamburger is bad for you.		

Read the paragraphs below.
Find one opinion in each paragraph.
Circle the opinion.

Bacteria help make yogurt.

Paragraph 1: Good Bacteria

Everybody thinks all bacteria are bad. But some bacteria are good. Some bacteria live in our stomach. This bacteria help the stomach break down food. Other bacteria produce vitamins that keep our bodies healthy. Bacteria also help make different kinds of food. For example, some bacteria turn milk sour. The sour milk is used to make yogurt.

Paragraph 2: Bacteria's Home

Bacteria can grow in many places. Most bacteria grow best in temperatures around 37°C. This temperature is the temperature of the human body. Some bacteria live in freezing temperatures, as low as 0°C. Other bacteria live in hot springs that are 90°C. Bacteria are the most interesting form of life in the world.

Bacteria can grow in hot springs.

Literacy Practice: Recipe

Recipes tell you how to cook food. Some recipes are clear. For example, the recipe will say, "Fry the onion for one minute."

But some recipes are unclear. For example, the recipe will say, "Fry the onion until it is soft." How soft is soft?

If a recipe is unclear, you might have to do a little guesswork.

© BigStockPhoto/Ryan Fox

Look at the recipe on the next page.
Answer these questions:

1. Read the ingredients. Underline any part that is unclear.
   Explain   (a) why these parts are unclear and
            (b) what you would do in each case if you were cooking this dish.

2. Read the instructions under Method. Underline any part that is unclear.
   Explain   (a) why the instructions are unclear and
            (b) what you would do in each case.

HEALTH

Chicken Vegetable Stir Fry

(Serves 4-6)

© BigStockPhoto/Sherri Camp

Ingredients

2 tablespoons cornstarch
1 cup chicken stock
3 tablespoons vegetable oil
1 onion, chopped in thick slices
3 cups broccoli, cut in pieces
1 red pepper, cut in thin strips
salt and pepper, to taste
3 cups chicken, cut in squares

Method

1. Combine cornstarch and chicken stock.
    Blend well. Set aside.

2. In a frying pan, heat 1½ tablespoons oil
    over medium-high heat. Add chicken.
    Stir-fry for 2 to 3 minutes, or until chicken
    meat is white. Transfer chicken to a plate.

3. Add remaining oil to frying pan. Add
    vegetables. Stir-fry 1 minute.

4. Add chicken stock mixture and cooked chicken
    pieces. Stir-fry until vegetables are tender-crisp.

5. Serve over hot rice.

Vocabulary

Read this sentence: Maya was *cautious* but she still got food poisoning.

The activities below help you understand the word *cautious*.
Follow the directions in each box.

cautious

1

Read the paragraphs below. As you read, try to figure out the meaning of *cautious*.

Maya checked the meat for green spots. She smelled it. The meat seemed okay. So why did Maya get sick? She had been so *cautious*.

• • • • •

The man on the phone said that Doreen won a trip. "Send us $35," said the man. "We will send you a plane ticket." Doreen thought, "This trip sounds to good to be true. I had better be *cautious*."

Now choose the correct meaning for cautious.

(a) angry

(b) careful

(c) surprised

2

Read about Myrna. She has a decision to make.

Myrna met Garth online. They sent each other emails for a few weeks. Then Garth invited Myrna to his place for dinner. "A couple of other friends are coming, too," said Garth.

Myrna decided to be cautious. What did she do? Circle the correct answer. Give a reason for your choice.

(a) Myrna told Garth she would rather meet for coffee at a cafe.

(b) Myrna baked an apple pie to bring to Garth's place.

(c) Myrna never emailed Garth again.

Word Attack 1: Predict the Word

Finish the sentences in the paragraph.
You can use any words that make sense.

Sometimes people use recipes when they cook. Recipes

tell you new ways to cook _____ ,

meat, and fish. Recipes list the _____

you need to buy. Recipes tell you how to _____ the meal.

Recipes use instruction words like combine, mix, and _____ .

> What do you do if you can't read a word?
>
> Active readers think of a word that makes sense.

Word Attack 2: Letter Patterns

Read the sentences.
Circle two words for each letter pattern.

ell

1. It's not enough just to smell leftover food.
2. You cannot tell if the food has bacteria.

ook

3. Make sure to cook food properly.
4. Look up times and temperatures.

aw

5. Thaw food in the fridge.
6. Do not leave raw meat, fish, and poultry at room temperature.

> Active readers look for letter patterns. A letter pattern looks and sounds the same. Say these words:
>
> **s**ound **r**ound **f**ound
>
> These words all have the same letter pattern.

Word Attack 3: Divide and Conquer

Read each sentence.
Circle the words that have a suffix.
The first one is an example.

1. Maya (checked) the meat for green spots.

2. Maya got stomach cramps.

3. She started throwing up.

4. Maya had food poisoning.

5. She learned about bacteria.

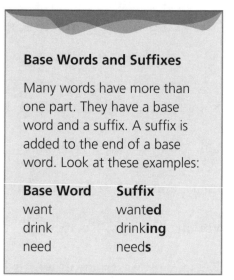

Base Words and Suffixes

Many words have more than one part. They have a base word and a suffix. A suffix is added to the end of a base word. Look at these examples:

Base Word	Suffix
want	want**ed**
drink	drink**ing**
need	need**s**

Read the paragraph.
Add suffixes to complete the words.
The first one is an example.

Cook food proper_ly___. Note cook_____

time_____ and temperature_____. Thaw food at

cold temperature_____. Keep vegetable_____ and

milk product_____ away from raw meat, poultry,

and fish.

Compound Words

Compound words are made from two or more little words.

butterfly   butter / fly

Read each sentence.
Find and divide the compound word.

1. Maya ate some leftover lunch meat.

2. She got food poisoning within 24 hours.

3. Lunchtime was a bad time for Maya.

Health
Skin Cancer

Vocabulary: expose

Mini-Lesson: Fact and Opinion

Literacy Practice: Product Label

▶▶ Discussion

Skin cancer is the most common type of cancer. Cases of skin cancer are on the rise. Do you worry about getting skin cancer? Why or why not?

Read the passage on the next two pages. Learn why Shanti was lucky.

Skin Cancer

Shanti had a small, red patch of skin on her back. She did not pay much attention to it. But her doctor did. The doctor sent Shanti to a skin doctor. The small red patch turned out to be skin cancer.

Shanti was lucky. She had a mild form of skin cancer, and her doctor caught the cancer early. So it was easy to remove. Other skin cancers can be deadly.

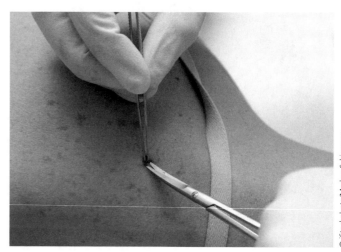

© iStockphoto/Markus Schiemann

Doctor checks for skin cancer.

Stop and Think:

Has a doctor ever checked your skin for cancer?

The main cause of skin cancer is the sun's UVB rays. If you need to be in the sun for more than 15 minutes, protect your skin. Did you know the sun's rays can pass through thin, white clothing? So wear dark colours and thick materials. Wear a hat made of thick cotton or canvas. The hat should have a wide brim to shade your face and neck. The sun's rays are strongest between 10 a.m. and 4 p.m., so be extra careful during these hours.

> **UVB rays:**
> (ultraviolet rays) rays from the sun that heat the skin; these rays can cause skin cancer

Stop and Think:

How else can you protect your skin from the sun? Read on. Are your ideas in the passage?

Do you feel safe from the sun on cloudy days? Do you feel safe sitting in the shade? The sun's harmful rays pass through clouds. The sun's rays also bounce off sand, water, snow, and concrete. So be careful. The sun will still find you on cloudy days—even in the shade of a tree.

> Do you use sunscreen? Some sunscreen may not be safe. Ask a pharmacist or doctor for advice.

Protecting your skin is important. You should also check your skin every few months. Look for changes in your skin. Is there a bump you have not seen before? Or a flat brown spot that looks like a scar? Do you feel any crusty or scaly patches? Have any moles or freckles changed colour, shape or feel? All these changes can be signs of skin cancer.

Don't take chances. Tell your doctor about any changes you notice in your skin. And always protect your skin from the sun.

▶▶ Check the Facts

1. Find three details about the sun's UVB rays. Check the passage to find the answer.

2. What is the most important idea in the passage?

   (a) Skin cancer can be deadly, so protect yourself.

   (b) Stay out of the sun.

▶▶ Discussion

1. Do you think people should protect themselves from the sun in the winter? Explain why or why not.

2. Did you protect yourself from the sun when you were young? Why or why not? Do you protect yourself now? Why or why not?

3. Babies and young children are at more risk of getting sunburn than adults. Give possible reasons why.

Mini-Lesson: Fact and Opinion

An opinion is a belief. It is a way of thinking about something. Sometimes an opinion is hard to prove.

Facts are different from opinions. Facts can be proven. A fact is 100 percent true.

Look at each pair of sentences.
Write F beside the sentence that is a fact.
Write O beside the sentence that is an opinion.

1. _____ Everyone hates bugs.

   _____ Some bugs fly.

2. _____ My birthday is in June.

   _____ June is the best month.

3. _____ Apples taste great.

   _____ Apples are good for you.

4. _____ My boss is very young.

   _____ My boss is 32 years old.

Look at the sentences.
Tick F for the sentences that are facts.
Tick O for the sentences that are opinions.

	F	O
1. Skin cancer is the most common type of cancer.		
2. Cloudy days make everyone sad.		
3. The sun's rays are strongest between 10 a.m. and 4 p.m.		
4. People worry too much about skin cancer.		
5. The main cause of cancer is the sun's UVB rays.		

Read the paragraphs below.
Find one opinion in each paragraph.
Circle the opinion.

Paragraph 1:
The Risk of Skin Cancer

Anyone can get skin cancer. But people with lighter skin are at more risk. Lighter skin does not protect as well from UVB rays. People who have a lot of moles are also at more risk. So are people with a history of skin cancer in the family. I believe people at risk will get skin cancer no matter what they do.

© BigStockPhoto/ScrappinStacy

Paragraph 2:
Children and Sunburn

Most parents do not protect their children from the sun. What should you do if a young child gets a sunburn? Cool the burned area in lukewarm water for at least 30 minutes. Put aloe vera cream on the burned area. A sunburn can cause shivers, so keep the child warm. Does the sunburn cause pain, blisters, or a rash? If yes, see a doctor.

© BigStockPhoto/Jane September

Literacy Practice: Product Label

Most products in drugstores have labels. Labels provide a lot of information. For example, labels tell us how to use a product. They also tell us what ingredients are in a product.

Some information on labels is hard to read. Sunscreen, for example, contains chemicals. Chemicals often have long names that are hard to read.

The label on page 57 is for sunscreen.
Use the label to answer these questions:

1. Read the information under **Uses** and **Directions**. Is the information clear? Write two questions you might ask the pharmacist.

   _____

   _____

2. Tick the information that appears under **Warnings**:

   (a) _____ what to do if sunscreen gets in your eyes

   (b) _____ what to do if you get a sunburn

   (c) _____ what to do if sunscreen causes a rash

   (d) _____ what to do if sunscreen is swallowed

▶▶ Discussion

3. (a) **Active Ingredients** make the product work. How can you find out if any of the active ingredients are unsafe?

   (b) Look at the **Ingredients**. Which words can you read? Underline them.

   (c) What might be one purpose of these ingredients? _____

4. Is it time to buy new sunscreen? Explain why or why not.

   (HINT: Look at the expiry date.)

Sunscreen Label

Uses: Protects against sunburn. Provides UVB/ UVA protection. Designed for use in water.

Directions: Apply 30 minutes before sun exposure. Reapply every 2 hours or after towel drying, swimming, or perspiring. **Children under 6 months of age:** ask a doctor

Warnings: For external use only. When using this product, keep out of eyes. Rinse with water to remove. Stop use and ask a doctor if a rash appears. **Keep out of reach of children.** If swallowed, get medical help or contact a Poison Control Centre right away.

Active Ingredients: Octinoxate 7.5%, Octisalate 5%, Oxybenzone 2.5%, Zinc Oxide 10%

Ingredients: Water, Lavender Extract, Neopentyl Glycol Diethylhexanoate, Polyglyceryl-4 Isostearate, Aloe Vera Leaf Juice, Glycerine, Pantenol, Orange Peel Extract, Cucumber Extract, Jejoba Seed Extract, Acetate, Sodium Chloride…

Expiry: 12/12/2014

Vocabulary

Read this sentence: Shanti *exposed* her back to the sun.

The activities below help you understand the word *expose*.
Follow the directions in each box.

expose

1

The word *expose* has many meanings. Here are three meanings of expose with example sentences:

(a) leave something with no cover or protection

Do not **expose** your skin to the sun for more than 15 minutes.

(b) introduce a person to something new

The teacher **exposed** the students to great works of art.

(c) let everyone know about something that is bad or hidden

At the end of the book, the writer **exposed** the killer.

Think of a new example sentence for each meaning of expose.

2

Read each paragraph. Match the meaning of expose with a meaning from Box 1. Write a, b, or c on the line.

1. _____ The robber was only 14 years old. He was protected by the law. News reports could not expose his name to the public.

2. _____ The bright red curtains were exposed to the sun. After five years, the curtains faded to a dull red.

3. _____ My new friend is from Mexico. She exposed me to the music in her culture. I am now a fan of pop singers in Mexico.

Word Attack 1: Predict the Word

Finish the sentences in the paragraph.
You can use any words that make sense.

Labels on cleaning products provide a lot of

information. A label lists the _____

that are found in the product. A label has

_____ so we know how to use the product. Some labels

tell us to keep the product away from young _____.

These cleaning products might be _____ .

What do you do if you can't read a word?

Active readers think of a word that makes sense.

Word Attack 2: Letter Patterns

Read the sentences.
Circle two words for each letter pattern.

all

1. The red spot was small.
2. I called the doctor to make an appointment.

atch

3. The doctor looked at the red patch.
4. "It is good to catch this early," she said.

eck

5. I check the skin on every part of my body.
6. I wear hats to protect my face and neck.

Active readers look for letter patterns. A letter pattern looks and sounds the same. Say these words:

sound   **r**ound   **f**ound

These words all have the same letter pattern.

Word Attack 3: Divide and Conquer

Read each sentence.
Circle the words that have a suffix.
The first one is an example.

1. (Protecting) your skin is important.

2. Check your skin every few months.

3. Look for changes in your skin.

4. Is there a spot that looks like a scar?

5. Do you feel any crusty patches?

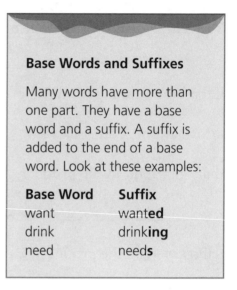

Base Words and Suffixes

Many words have more than one part. They have a base word and a suffix. A suffix is added to the end of a base word. Look at these examples:

Base Word	Suffix
want	want**ed**
drink	drink**ing**
need	need**s**

Read the paragraph.
Add suffixes to complete the words.
The first one is an example.

Do you feel safe from the sun on cloud_y___

day_____? Do you feel safe sitting under

tree_____? The sun's harmful ray_____ pass

through cloud_____. The ray_____ also bounce

off sand, water, snow, and concrete.

© BigStockPhoto/Onebuck!

Read each sentence.
Find and divide the compound word.

1. Sunscreen is not always safe.

2. I don't want to get a sunburn.

3. I should buy a pair of sunglasses.

Compound Words

Compound words are made from two or more little words.

butterfly   butter / fly

Environment
Deepwater

© Greenpeace

Vocabulary: liable

Mini-Lesson: Cause and Effect

Literacy Practice: Pie Graph

© iStockphoto/Eyeidea

▶▶ Discussion

Oil rigs drill deep wells under the ocean floor. The rigs pump oil from the well. Do you think it is a good idea to drill for oil in the ocean? Why or why not?

In April, 2010, an oil rig off the coast of the US caught on fire. The fire killed 11 men and hurt 17 others. The name of the oil rig was Deepwater Horizon.

Read the passage on the next two pages. Learn what happened after the Deepwater Horizon caught on fire.

Deepwater

Workers heard a thump, then a hissing sound. The huge oil rig shook. A stream of seawater, mud, and gas blew out of the well. The oil rig exploded and caught on fire. The rig burned for 36 hours, and then sank. As the rig sank, the main pipe to the oil well broke. The well started to gush oil into the sea.

The Deepwater Horizon on fire.

The oil rig was the Deepwater Horizon. BP, a British oil company, was renting the rig. The US government blamed BP for the disaster. The government said BP cut corners to save money. BP blamed Transocean, a US company that built and owned the rig. BP said safety equipment on the rig failed to work. Transocean blamed working crews.

For weeks, BP tried to stop the oil from gushing out of the well. The oil spread and moved toward the US coast. It killed hundreds of turtles, seabirds, and dolphins along the way. The oil washed into marshes and wetlands full of plant and water life.

> The oil well was 1,500 metres below the sea. It was 80 kilometres off the east coast of the US.

Stop and Think:

Why do you think the animals died from the oil?

The oil also washed onto the beaches. Many tourist towns lost money and jobs. Fishing areas were shut down. People who made money from shrimp, oysters, and crabs lost their jobs.

> The oil spill was large. A person would have had to walk 15 days and nights to get around it.

Stop and Think:

Why would tourist towns lose jobs because of the oil spill?

ENVIRONMENT

People used every way possible to clean up the oil. Workers used boats to lay miles of floating booms. The booms helped to stop the oil from spreading. Skimmer boats sucked the oil off the water. The ocean was set on fire to burn off some of the oil. BP used chemicals to break down the oil. Some experts said the chemicals made the oil more toxic.

At last, BP managed to set a giant cap on top of the well. BP then plugged the well with heavy mud and cement. After three long months, the oil finally stopped flowing. The cleanup continues.

© Greenpeace

▶▶ Check the Facts

1. How did the Deepwater Horizon oil spill affect (a) the environment and (b) the people? Check the passage to find the answers.

2. What is the most important message in the passage?

(a) The Deepwater oil spill caused a lot of damage.

(b) The Deepwater oil rig exploded.

▶▶ Discussion

1. Why do you think the companies and the government started to play the "blame game"?

2. Imagine a huge oil spill happened along the coast of Canada. Would the oil spill affect you? Why or why not? If yes, explain how.

3. People use oil and gas every day. For example, oil and gas are used to air condition homes. How else do people use oil and gas? How can people cut down on using oil and gas?

Mini-Lesson: Cause and Effect

Good writers use a plan to develop their ideas. One kind of plan is cause and effect. Active readers look for the writer's plan. Knowing the plan helps readers understand the writer's ideas.

Look at the idea map below.
Answer the questions that follow.

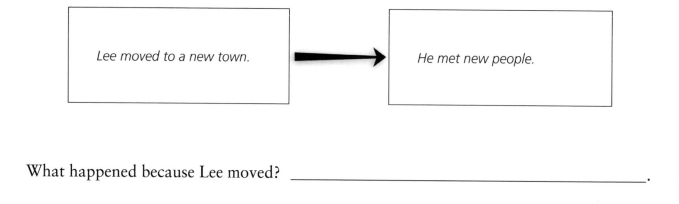

What happened because Lee moved? _____.

Why did Lee meet new people? _____.

The idea map above shows a connection between two ideas.
The idea in the first box is the **cause**. A cause makes something happen.
The idea in the second box is the **effect**. An effect is the thing that happens.

Look at the idea map below. Add an effect that makes sense.

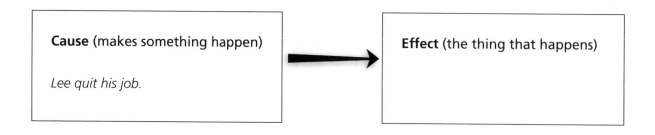

Sometimes one cause can have more than one effect.

Look at Idea Map 1.
What is the cause?
How many effects does the cause have?

Idea Map 1

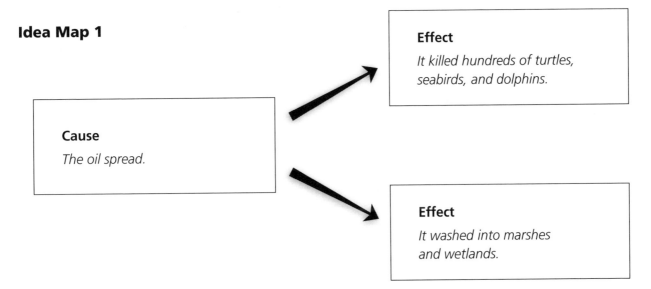

Cause

The oil spread.

Effect

It killed hundreds of turtles, seabirds, and dolphins.

Effect

It washed into marshes and wetlands.

Read the paragraph below.
Finish Idea Map 2.

The oil washed onto the beaches. Tourist towns lost money and jobs. Fishing areas were shut down.

Idea Map 2

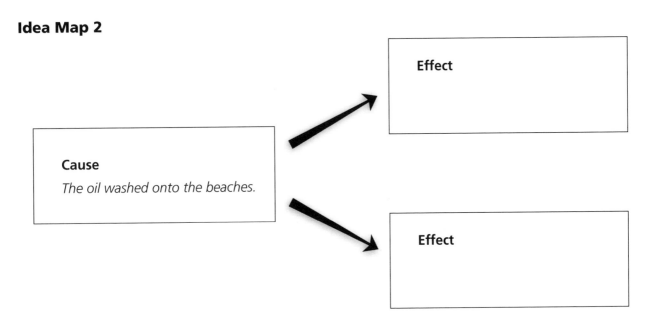

Cause

The oil washed onto the beaches.

Effect

Effect

Literacy Practice: Pie Graph

Pie graphs provide information. Pie graphs look like a piece of pie cut up into pieces. The whole pie, or graph, equals 100 percent (100%). Each piece shows a percentage of the whole pie graph.

Pie graphs have a title. They also have text. The text explains the information in the graph.

Look at the pie graph below.
Answer the questions on page 67.

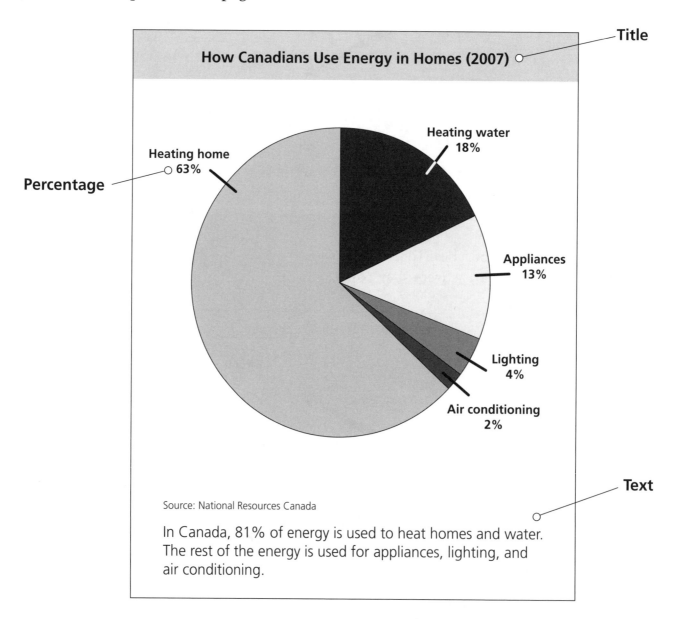

How Canadians Use Energy in Homes (2007) — Title

Heating water 18%

Heating home 63% — Percentage

Appliances 13%

Lighting 4%

Air conditioning 2%

Source: National Resources Canada

In Canada, 81% of energy is used to heat homes and water. The rest of the energy is used for appliances, lighting, and air conditioning. — Text

ENVIRONMENT

1. What is the **title** of the pie graph?

   _____

2. What **percentage** of total energy do Canadians use to

   (a) light their homes? _____

   (b) run stoves, fridges, microwaves, etc.? _____

3. (a) What percentage of total energy do Canadians use for heating? _____

   (b) How did you figure out the answer?

   _____

4. Why do you think the percentage of total energy use is so low for air conditioning?

   _____

5. (a) List 10 things you did today in your home that used energy.

   1. _____   6. _____

   2. _____   7. _____

   3. _____   8. _____

   4. _____   9. _____

   5. _____   10. _____

   (b) Where do each of your activities go on the pie graph?

   Write the number in the correct piece of the pie graph.

   (c) Which piece of the pie graph has the most numbers? Does this surprise you?
   Why or why not?

Vocabulary

Read this sentence: The company was *liable* for the damage to the environment.

The activities below help you understand the word *liable*.
Follow the directions in each box.

liable

1

The word *liable* has many meanings. Here are three meanings of liable with example sentences:

(a) responsible by law to take the blame for something

The landlord never shovels the snow. He will be **liable** if any tenants slip and hurt themselves.

(b) likely to do something

I'm **liable** to lose my temper when I am tired.

(c) likely to be hurt by something in some way

Smokers are more **liable** to get cancer than non-smokers.

Think of a new example sentence for each meaning of liable.

2

Read each paragraph. Match the meaning of liable with a meaning from Box 1. Write a, b, or c on the line.

1. _____ Don't tease the dog! He's liable to bite you if he gets mad.

2. _____ Older people need to be careful. They are more liable than young people to break a hip bone.

3. _____ Do not co-sign a loan. If the person does not pay back the loan, you will be liable for paying it back.

Word Attack 1: Predict the Word

Finish the sentences in the paragraph.
You can use any words that make sense.

People use energy every day. They use energy such as

_____ and gas. People use more energy

in the _____ than in the summer. They

use energy to heat their _____. They

also use energy to run appliances like ovens, fridges, and

_____.

> What do you do if you can't read a word?
>
> Active readers think of a word that makes sense.

Word Attack 2: Letter Patterns

Read the sentences.
Circle two words for each letter pattern.

ain

1. The main pipe to the oil well broke.
2. The oil was like a big stain on the ocean.

each

3. The oil reached the coast of the US.
4. The oil washed onto the beaches.

> Active readers look for letter patterns. A letter pattern looks and sounds the same. Say these words:
>
> **s**ound **r**ound **f**ound
>
> These words all have the same letter pattern.

own

5. Tourist towns lost money.
6. The number of jobs went down.

Word Attack 3: Divide and Conquer

Read each sentence.
Circle the words that have a suffix.
The first one is an example.

1. The oil (killed) hundreds of turtles.

2. It killed seabirds and dolphins.

3. The oil washed into marshes and wetlands.

4. Fishing areas shut down.

5. The oil affected shrimp, oysters, and crabs.

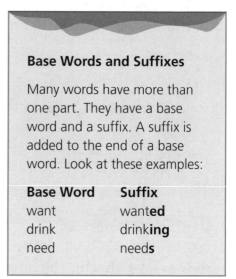

Base Words and Suffixes

Many words have more than one part. They have a base word and a suffix. A suffix is added to the end of a base word. Look at these examples:

Base Word	Suffix
want	want**ed**
drink	drink**ing**
need	need**s**

Read the paragraph.
Add suffixes to complete the words.
The first one is an example.

Work_ers_ used boat_____ to lay mile_____ of

float_____ boom_____. The boom_____ help_____

to stop the oil from spread_____. Skimmer

boat_____ suck_____ the oil off the water.

BP used chemical_____ to break down the oil.

© Greenpeace

Read each sentence.
Find and divide the compound word.

1. Seawater, mud, and gas blew out of the well.

2. The Deepwater Horizon caught on fire.

3. The oil washed into wetlands and marshes.

Compound Words

Compound words are made from two or more little words.

butterfly   butter / fly

Environment

The Cleanup

Vocabulary: optimistic

Mini-Lesson: Cause and Effect

Literacy Practice: Utility Bill

© BigStockPhoto/Yuri Gupta

▶▶ Discussion

Every dark cloud has a silver lining.

What does this sentence mean to you? Do you agree with what the sentence says?

Read the passage on the next two pages. Learn what the silver lining was in the Deepwater oil spill.

The Cleanup

Did you know that human hair was used to clean up the Deepwater oil spill? Hair is like a sponge. It soaks up all kinds of liquid, including oil. And hair floats, even when it is soaked with oil.

A non-profit group came up with the idea of making "hair booms." Volunteers made the hair booms from pantyhose stuffed with human hair and fur. People from around the world heard about the hair booms. Hair salons sent in tons of cut hair. Pet groomers and sheep farmers sent in fur.

Volunteers made hair booms.

Stop and Think:

How do you think people heard about the hair booms?

Big oil spills have far-reaching effects. People lose jobs. Sea animals and birds suffer and die. Beaches and wetlands turn black with oil. But something good happens, too. People come together.

During the Deepwater oil spill, some experts offered their skills for free. For example, scientists and vets rescued sea turtles. The turtles had breathed in toxic oil fumes. They had swallowed oily water. So the turtles were sick and not eating. The experts knew how to remove the toxic oil from the turtles' bodies. They fed the turtles mayo and vegetable oil. Many turtles got better and gained weight. These turtles were set free.

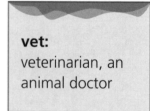

vet:
veterinarian, an animal doctor

Not all people had the right skills to offer. But many people were able to offer their time. Some people joined a volunteer group called Coast Watch. Coast watchers walked along the coast. They looked for plants and animals covered in oil. They looked for patches of oil on beaches. The coast watchers took notes. Some took pictures and videos. Then the coast watchers phoned a hotline to make a report.

mayo:
mayonnaise

ENVIRONMENT

Stop and Think:

**Would you like to be a coast watcher?
Why or why not?**

Disasters can make us feel helpless. But finding a way to help, even a little, brings a promise of hope. Sometimes, getting a haircut is all it takes.

. . . .

▶▶ Check the Facts

1. Experts rescued sea turtles. Find two other ways people helped during the Deepwater oil spill. Check the passage to find the answer.

2. What is the most important idea in the passage?

   (a) Some people could not help during the oil spill. They had no skills.

   (b) People helped in many different ways during the oil spill.

▶▶ Discussion

1. People who love animals might volunteer as coast watchers. What other people might volunteer as coast watchers?

2. Think about the last time you and others had to solve a problem. Describe the experience. What were you able to offer? Skills? Time? Labour?

3. Where can you find out about volunteer work in your community? What kind of volunteer work would you like to do? Explain why.

Mini-Lesson: Cause and Effect

Good writers use a plan to develop their ideas. One kind of plan is cause and effect. The **cause** makes something happen. The **effect** is the thing that happens.

Read the paragraphs below.
Finish the cause and effect idea maps.

Paragraph 1   Scientists and vets rescued sea turtles. The turtles had breathed in toxic oil fumes. They had swallowed oily water. So the turtles were sick and not eating.

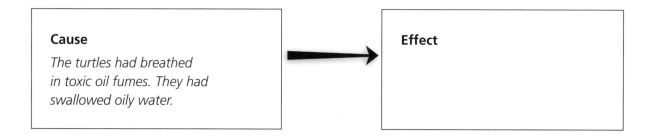

Cause

The turtles had breathed in toxic oil fumes. They had swallowed oily water.

Effect

Paragraph 2   The experts knew how to remove the toxic oil from the turtles' bodies. They fed the turtles mayo and vegetable oil. Many turtles got better and gained weight.

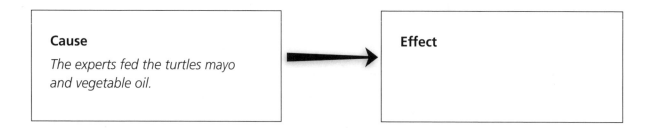

Cause

The experts fed the turtles mayo and vegetable oil.

Effect

Paragraph 3

Big oil spills have far-reaching effects. People lose jobs. Sea animals and birds suffer and die. Beaches and wetlands turn black with oil. But something good happens, too. People come together.

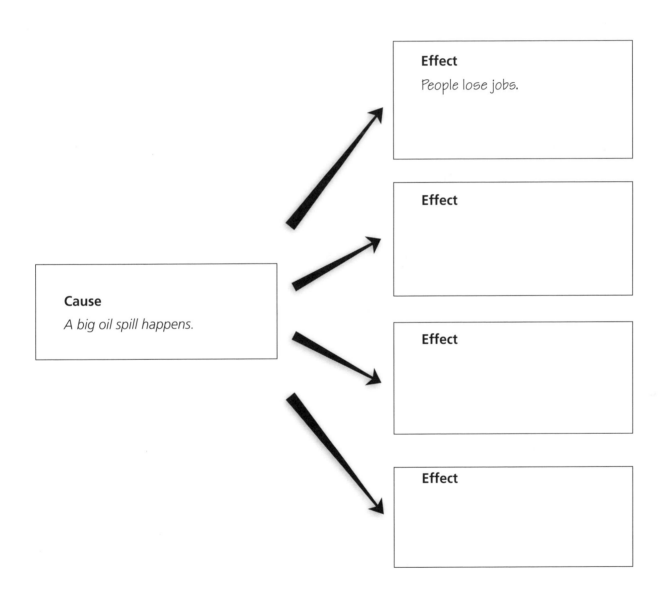

Cause

A big oil spill happens.

Effect

People lose jobs.

Effect

Effect

Effect

Literacy Practice: Utility Bill

Which of these bills do you pay each month? Water? Electricity? Gas? These bills are called utility bills.

Utility bills show a lot of information. For example, they show how much you owe. They show how much you paid on your last bill. And they show penalty costs for late payments.

Imagine you get the utility bill below.
Answer the questions on page 77.

ABC UTILITY COMPANY

Statement Date: July 22, 2010

Account Number: 55631411-A

Your Name
123 Main St.
Big Town, Canada, A1A 1A1

Questions?   Call 555-5555
                      1-800-555-5555

Monday to Friday: 8 am – 8 pm
Saturday: 8 am – 5 pm

Home service/Repairs:
    Power: (555) 555-3333
    Water: (555) 555-2222

Amount of last bill:	$86.50
Payment received:	- 40.00
Balance	46.50
Penalty for late payment	1.16
New Charges:	93.82

Electric Energy	59.03
GST (5%)	2.95
Water	26.20
Drainage	5.64

Total payment now due   **$ 141.48**

(Payment after August 12, 2010: $ 145.02)

1. Who sent you this utility bill? _____

2. In what month did they send you the bill? _____

3. What was the amount of your last bill? _____

4. How much do you still owe on your last bill?

   (a) $46.50   (b) $1.16   (c) $47.66

5. What costs more?   (a) electricity   (b) water

6. Your new charges for July are $93.82. Why do you owe $141.48?

   _____

7. You pay off the bill on August 15, 2010. You want your balance to be zero. How much do you pay?

   (a) $141.48   (b) $145.02   (c) $46.50

8. How much time does this company give you to pay your bill penalty-free?

   (a) about ten days   (b) about three weeks   (c) one month

9. (a) Your water shuts off on Saturday at 3:00 p.m.
      What number do you call for help?

   _____

   (b) The service person asks you for your account number.
      What number do you give him?

   _____

Vocabulary

Read this sentence: The *optimistic* volunteers made hair booms.

The activities below help you understand the word *optimistic*.
Follow the directions in each box.

optimistic

1

Read the paragraphs below. As you read, try to figure out the meaning of *optimistic*.

The oil spill caused a lot of damage. But I was *optimistic*. People come together in times of trouble. They find a way to make things better.

• • • • •

"It will never stop raining," cried the little girl. "Yes, it will," said her *optimistic* mother. "Look! I can see a rainbow just over there."

Now choose the correct meaning for optimistic.

(a) believing that good things will happen

(b) believing that bad things will happen

2

1. What would an optimistic person say? Tick three of the following sentences.

   1. _____ I give up!

   2. _____ Let's look at the bright side of things.

   3. _____ Don't worry. Things will get better.

   4. _____ There's no way we can change things.

   5. _____ Life is not fair!

   6. _____ I just know something good is going to happen today.

2. Think of a person you know that is optimistic. What words would you use to describe this person? How do you feel when you are around this person?

Word Attack 1: Predict the Word

Finish the sentences in the paragraph.
You can use any words that makes sense.

Most people hate paying utility bills. People have to pay

utility bills every _____. People pay for

services like water and _____. All utility

bills have your name and _____ on them.

Utility bills also have a _____ to call if

you need help.

> What do you do if you can't read a word?
>
> Active readers think of a word that makes sense.

Word Attack 2: Letter Patterns

Read the sentences.
Circle two words for each letter pattern.

oat

1. Hair floats even when it is heavy with oil.
2. People used small boats to lay the booms.

ill

3. Big oil spills have far-reaching effects.
4. The oil can kill plants and animals.

> Active readers look for letter patterns. A letter pattern looks and sounds the same. Say these words:
>
> **s**ound **r**ound **f**ound
>
> These words all have the same letter pattern.

ope

5. Helping in a disaster can give people hope.
6. People cope with disasters in many ways.

Word Attack 3: Divide and Conquer

Read each sentence.
Circle the words that have a suffix.

1. Some people (joined) a volunteer group.

2. The group was called Coast Watch.

3. Coast watchers walked along the coast.

4. They walked along the beaches.

5. They looked for animals covered in oil.

Base Words and Suffixes

Many words have more than one part. They have a base word and a suffix. A suffix is added to the end of a base word. Look at these examples:

Base Word	Suffix
want	want**ed**
drink	drink**ing**
need	need**s**

Read the paragraph.
Add suffixes to complete the words.

The coast watchers took note_s___. Some took

picture_____ and video_____. Then the coast

watch_____ phone_____ a hotline. Disaster_____

can make us feel helpless. But find_____ a way to

help bring_____ a promise of hope.

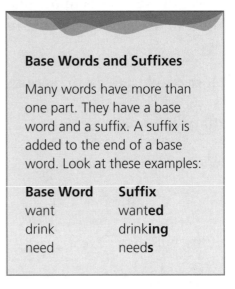

© BigStockPhoto/Chrissie Shepherd

Read each sentence.
Find and divide the compound word.

1. The cleanup will take many years.

2. Coast Watchers phoned a hotline.

3. Just getting a haircut can help.

Compound Words

Compound words are made from two or more little words.

butterfly   butter / fly

ENVIRONMENT

History
Workers' Rights

© Archives of Manitoba

Vocabulary: mediate

Mini-Lesson: Timeline

Literacy Practice: Pay Stub

© iStockphoto/Jim Jurica

▶▶ Discussion

Sometimes workers are not happy in their jobs. How can workers create change in a workplace?

Some workplaces have a union. A union is a group that protects workers' rights. Workers become members of the union. Sometimes the members of the union vote to go on strike.

In 1919, workers in Winnipeg went on strike. This strike was the biggest strike in Canada's history.

Read the passage on the next two pages. Learn why the workers went on strike.

Workers' Rights

The First World War ended in 1918. Canadian men came home. But they came home to hard times. Jobs were few. The cost of living was up by 75 percent.

In Winnipeg, workers asked for better working conditions. They wanted a living wage and an 8-hour workday. But employers would not listen. So two large unions voted to go on strike.

Strikers march by the city hall, 1919.

© Library and Archives Canada/C-34022

Stop and Think:

What do you think a "living wage" means?

On May 15, Winnipeg shut down. Workers walked out of plants. They walked out of stores and banks. Even police and firemen walked off the job. Streetcars stopped running. Mail and phone service stopped. Water and power supplies were cut off. Workers from every union in Winnipeg joined the strike. Within hours, 30,000 workers across the city were on strike.

Business owners and politicians were against the strike. They set up a group to fight the striking workers. This group fired the police. They hired 2,000 "special" police.

The federal government also wanted to break the strike. The government gave postal workers a choice. Go back to work or be fired. They also changed laws. Now it was easy to arrest strikers. Ten strike leaders went to jail.

On Saturday, June 21, crowds of workers filled the streets downtown. The Mounted Police charged them on horses. The special police chased the workers into back streets, clubs in hand. The army came with machine guns. One person was

> The group was called the Citizens' Committee of 1000.

> All postal workers work for the federal government.

killed and 30 were hurt. The day came to be known as Bloody Saturday. On June 26, the strike leaders ended the strike. They feared more violence.

Stop and Think:

Why do you think the strike leaders feared more violence?

Some people feel the strike failed. Many workers gained nothing and lost much. Others do not agree. They feel the strike led to better working conditions. One thing is sure. The people in power could no longer ignore the workers' voice.

· · · · · · · · · · · · · · · · · ·

▶▶ Check the Facts

1. Which groups of people were against the strike? Check the passage to find the answer.

2. What is the most important idea in the passage?

   (a) Workers were killed and injured during Bloody Saturday.

   (b) The Winnipeg General Strike gave workers a voice.

▶▶ Discussion

1. Why do you think the federal government wanted to break the strike?

2. Imagine you lived in Winnipeg in 1919. How would you be affected by the strike?

3. What would you want to change in your workplace? Would you strike for these changes? Explain why or why not.

Mini-Lesson: Timeline

Good writers use a plan to develop their ideas. One kind of plan is a timeline. Writers use timelines to put events in the order that they happen. Active readers look for the writer's plan. Knowing the plan helps readers understand the writer's ideas.

Look at the timeline below.
It tells the history of the Winnipeg General Strike.
Answer the questions that follow.

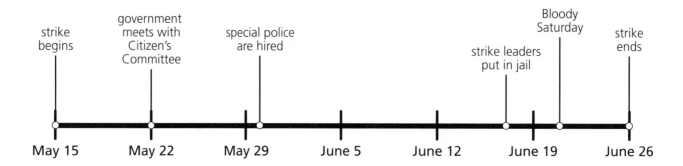

1. The first dates on the timeline are May 15 and May 22. What is the length of time between these two dates?

   (a) 1 day   (b) 1 week   (c) 1 month

2. (a) When did the strike start? _____   (b) When did it end? _____

   (c) How many weeks did the strike last? _____

   How did you figure out the answer?

3. Bloody Saturday was June 21. How long after Bloody Saturday did the strike end?

   (a) 1 week after   (b) less than a week after   (c) more than a week after

Labour Day

Everyone likes a long weekend. Many
workers get a holiday on the first Monday
of September. This Monday is called
Labour Day.

**Look at the timeline below.
It tells the history of Labour Day.
Answer the questions that follow.**

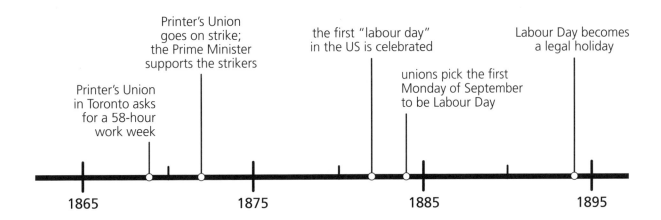

1. The first two years marked on the timeline are 1865 and 1875. Put an X on the
    timeline to show the year 1870. How did you figure out where to put the X?

2. When did the Printer's Union ask for a strike?   (a) 1869   (b) 1871

    How did you figure out the answer?

3. (a) In what year did the unions pick a day to be Labour Day? _____

    (b) How many years later did Labour Day become a national holiday?

    (i) 5   (ii) 10   (iii) 15

    How did you figure out the answer?

4. The history of Labour Day begins in 1869. About how many years did it take
    for Labour Day to become a legal holiday?

    (a) 15   (ii) 25   (c) 35

Literacy Practice: Pay Stub

How do you get paid at work? Most people get paid by cheque. A cheque has two parts: the part you cash and the part you keep for your records. The part you keep for your records is called a pay stub.

Look at Leon's pay stub on page 87.
Answer these questions:

1. Leon works at _____ .

2. The **pay period** is from November 1 to _____ .

3. The pay period covers   (a) 1 week   (b) 2 weeks   (c) 1 month

4. You need to add up all hours worked to get **gross earnings.** The hours include regular pay, vacation pay, and _____ pay.

5. The biggest **deduction** is _____ .

6. The **net pay** on this pay stub is $_____ .

7. How many hours (hrs) did Leon work during this pay period?
   (a) 64   (b) 68   (c) 84

8. What would be Leon's gross earnings with no overtime?
   (a) $672.55   (b) $920.00   (c) $800.00

9. Find the total for gross earnings. Copy it here: $_____

   Find the total for deductions. Copy it here: $_____

   How do you use these two totals to figure out net pay?

   (a) add the two totals together

   (b) subtract deductions from gross earnings

Pay Stub

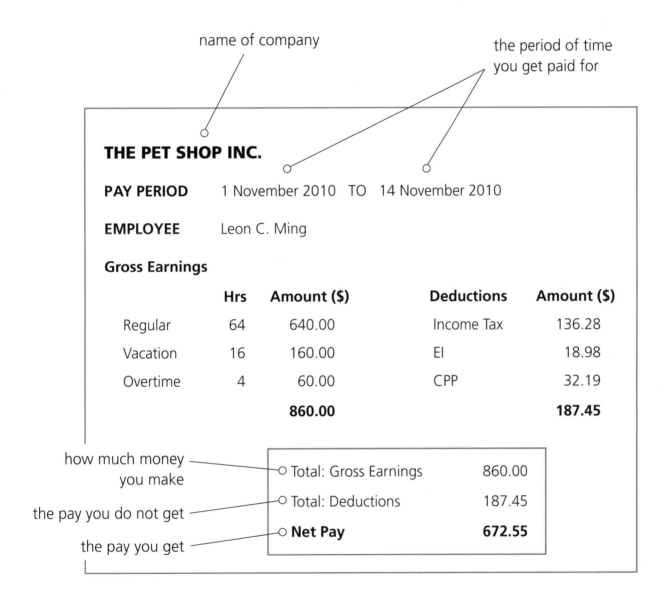

name of company

the period of time you get paid for

THE PET SHOP INC.

PAY PERIOD   1 November 2010   TO   14 November 2010

EMPLOYEE   Leon C. Ming

Gross Earnings

	Hrs	Amount ($)	Deductions	Amount ($)
Regular	64	640.00	Income Tax	136.28
Vacation	16	160.00	EI	18.98
Overtime	4	60.00	CPP	32.19
		860.00		**187.45**

how much money you make

the pay you do not get

the pay you get

Total: Gross Earnings	860.00
Total: Deductions	187.45
Net Pay	**672.55**

Vocabulary

Read this sentence: He's a good listener, so the two groups asked him to *mediate*.

The activities below help you understand the word *mediate*.
Follow the directions in each box.

mediate

1

Read the paragraphs below. As you read, try to figure out the meaning of *mediate*.

Winston had to *mediate* between the union and the company. Both sides agreed to a 3 percent raise in pay. Both sides were happy.

• • • • •

I argue with my sister a lot. Sometimes we argue for a long time. Then my dad steps in to *mediate*. He always finds a way to please us both.

Now choose the correct meaning for mediate.

(a) help two people, or groups of people, reach an agreement

(b) pick a side to support

2

Read about Norm. He has a problem.

Norm and Tracy are getting married. Norm's family wants a big, fancy wedding. Tracy wants a small wedding. Norm's family and Tracy are not speaking to each other.

What should Norm do to mediate between his wife and parents? Circle the correct answer. Explain your choice.

(a) invite both sides to sit down and listen to one another

(b) convince Tracy to elope

(c) tell his family they will have to pay all the costs for a big wedding

Word Attack 1: Predict the Word

Finish the sentences in the paragraph.
You can use any words that make sense.

A pay stub shows how many hours you work. It also

shows how much _____ you make.

A pay stub can cover a time period of one or two

_____, or even a month. The time period

depends on how often your _____ pays

you.

> What do you do if you can't read a word?
>
> Active readers think of a word that makes sense.

Word Attack 2: Letter Patterns

Read the sentences.
Circle two words for each letter pattern.

ike

1. Workers did not like working conditions.
2. They went on strike.

ail

3. Mail and phone service shut down.
4. Ten strike leaders landed in jail.

> Active readers look for letter patterns. A letter pattern looks and sounds the same. Say these words:
>
> **s**ound **r**ound **f**ound
>
> These words all have the same letter pattern.

eet

5. The strikers ran into side streets.
6. Who did they meet? The special police.

Word Attack 3: Divide and Conquer

Read each sentence.
Circle the words that have a suffix.
The first one is an example.

1. (Employers) did not listen to the workers.

2. Members in two unions went on strike.

3. Other unions joined the strike.

4. The unions asked the CSC to help.

5. Strike leaders ended the strike.

Read the paragraph.
Add suffixes to complete the words.
The first one is an example.

Crowd*s*____ of work____ fill____ the

street____. The special police chase____ the

work____ into back street____ . The army

came with machine gun____. One person

was kill____ and 30 were hurt.

Read each sentence.
Find and divide the compound word.

1. Workers filled the streets downtown.

2. They wanted an 8-hour workday.

3. Now workers get paid overtime.

Base Words and Suffixes

Many words have more than one part. They have a base word and a suffix. A suffix is added to the end of a base word. Look at these examples:

Base Word	Suffix
want	want**ed**
drink	drink**ing**
need	need**s**

© Archives of Manitoba

Police clear the streets.

Compound Words

Compound words are made from two or more little words.

butterfly   butter / fly

© CP images 2009

History
Father of Medicare

Vocabulary: reform

Mini-Lesson: Timeline

Literacy Practice: Table

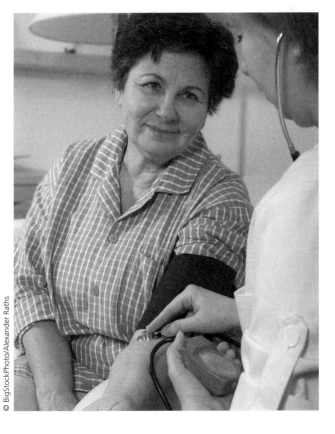

© BigStockPhoto/Alexander Raths

▶▶ Discussion

In Canada, all people have an equal chance to get good health care.

Do you think this sentence is true? Why or why not?

Tommy Douglas was born in 1904 in Scotland. Forty years later, he was the premier of Saskatchewan. People call him the "Father of Medicare." The medicare system helps people with their health care costs.

Read the passage on the next two pages. Find out why people call Tommy Douglas the Father of Medicare.

Father of Medicare

When Tommy Douglas was ten, he almost lost his leg to bone disease. His family could not pay for a doctor. But Tommy got lucky. A doctor agreed to work on Tommy's leg for free. Tommy's leg was saved.

Tommy runs for office.

In 1919, Tommy and his family moved to Winnipeg. That spring, he watched a workers' strike, where he saw police beat up and shoot workers. He never forgot that brutal moment. He was 14 years old.

Stop and Think:

Imagine you are Tommy watching the police. What are you thinking? What do you feel?

Tommy did not finish high school. He quit school to help support his family. He went back to school at age 20 and became a minister. He got married and moved to Saskatchewan. The Great Depression had just started. Tommy had work as a minister. But many other people were homeless and hungry. Many families lost their farms.

In 1934, Tommy went into politics. He helped start a political party called the CCF. In 1944, Tommy became premier of Saskatchewan. He was premier for 17 years. In that time, Tommy and the CCF worked hard. They made lives better for all people.

Tommy's main goal was to create medicare. But the road to change was not easy. The doctors were afraid they would make less money with medicare. The doctors went on strike for almost three weeks. But the doctors were no match for Tommy Douglas. By 1962, all people in Saskatchewan had the right to a doctor and full health care.

> The **Great Depression** was worldwide. It lasted from 1929 to 1939. Jobs were few.

> **CCF**: (Cooperative Commonwealth Federation) a political party that helped farmers and working people.

Stop and Think:

What do you think full heath care means?

The CCF also made laws for better working conditions. The minimum wage went up. The hours of work went down to 44 a week. Workers could get two weeks of paid vacation a year.

Tommy's early life shaped his beliefs. He knew what it was like to grow up on the wrong side of the tracks. In 2004, people voted Tommy Douglas the greatest Canadian in history.

In 1966, the federal government created a national medicare plan.

Tommy Douglas died of cancer in 1986.

....

▶▶ Check the Facts

1. How did Tommy's early life shape his beliefs? Check the passage to find the answer.

2. What is the most important idea in the passage?

   (a) Tommy Douglas is an important person in the history of Canada's health care system.

   (b) Tommy Douglas liked politics.

▶▶ Discussion

1. Why do you think Tommy left the ministry to enter politics?

2. Tommy Douglas's work led to many changes. Do you think his work has helped you and your family? Give specific examples.

3. Canada has a public health care system. Do you think there should also be a private health care system? Why or why not?

Mini-Lesson: Timeline

Good writers use a plan to develop their ideas. One kind
of plan is a timeline. Writers use timelines to put ideas in
the order that they happen.

**Look at the timeline below. It shows Tommy Douglas's life.
Answer the questions that follow.**

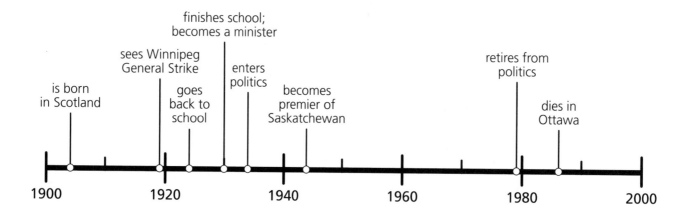

1. Find the years 1900 and 1920 on the timeline. Put an X on the timeline
   to show the year 1910. How did you figure out the answer?

2. When did Tommy finish school? _____

   Was the answer hard to figure out? Why or why not?

3. (a) About when did Tommy enter politics? _____

   (b) About when did Tommy retire from politics? _____

   (c) About how many years was Tommy in politics? _____

   Was it hard to figure out the answers for 3 (a), (b), or (c)?
   Why or why not?

Viola Desmond

What do you remember about Viola Desmond? The timeline below shows important events in Viola's life. Use the timeline to answer the questions that follow.

© 2010 Richard Rudnicki. Reprinted with permission of Groundwood Books Ltd.

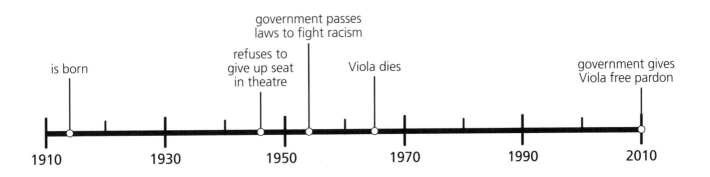

1. Find the years 1910 and 1930 on the timeline. Put an X on the timeline to show the year 1920.

   About when was Viola born? _____ How did you figure out the answer?

2. Put an X on the timeline to show the year 1960.

   (a) When did Viola die? _____ How did you figure out the answer?

   (b) About how many years later did the government pardon Viola? _____

   How did you figure out the answer?

3. Mark on the timeline the year you were born. How does your year of birth connect to an event in Viola's life? (Example: I was born ten years after the government in Nova Scotia passed laws against racism.)

Literacy Practice: Table

People use tables to organize facts. Tables have a title and headings. The title and headings show how the facts are organized.

Some tables have a key. The key explains the symbols in the table. One example of a symbol is a check mark (✔). Some tables use short forms to save space. For example, the short form of *British Columbia* is *BC*.

Look at the table on page 97. Then answer these questions:

1. What is the **title** of the table?

   _____

2. Look at the **headings**. Find the short forms for the following provinces and territory:

   (a) Saskatchewan _____   (b) Quebec _____   (c) Yukon Territory _____

3. Look at the list of holidays in the first column. Find Remembrance Day.
   When is Remembrance Day? _____

4 (a) How many symbols are in the **key?** _____

   (b) Which symbol shows that a workplace might *not* give a holiday? _____

5. All workplaces in Canada must give four holidays. Circle the holidays.

6. Mark the following statements true (T) or false (F).

   (a) Workers in Yukon Territory have a day off for Victoria Day. _____

   (b) All workplaces in Quebec give Good Friday as a holiday. _____

   (c) Over half of workplaces in Canada give Thanksgiving as a holiday. _____

7. Find your province or territory. Which holidays must workers get?

Holidays in Canada

Title
Headings

Name of Holiday	Day of Holiday	BC	AB	SK	MB	ON	QC	NB	NS	PE	NL	YT	NT	NU
New Year's Day	January 1	✓	✓	✓	✓	✓	✓	✓	✓	✓	✓	✓	✓	✓
Family Day	Third Monday in February	✓	✓	✓		✓								
Good Friday	Friday before Easter Sunday	✓	✓	✓	✓	✓	*	✓	✓	✓	✓	✓	✓	✓
Easter Monday	Monday after Easter Sunday						✓							
Victoria Day	Monday coming before May 25	✓	✓	✓	✓	✓	✓	*	*	✓	*	✓	✓	✓
Canada Day	July 1	✓	✓	✓	✓	✓	✓	✓	✓	✓	✓	✓	✓	✓
Civic Holiday	First Monday in August	✓	*	*	✓	*	*	✓	*	*	*	*	*	✓
Labour Day	First Monday in September	✓	✓	✓	✓	✓	✓	✓	✓	✓	✓	✓	✓	✓
Thanksgiving	Second Monday in October	✓	✓	✓	✓	✓	✓	*	*	*	*	✓	✓	✓
Remembrance Day	November 11	✓	✓	✓	*	*	*	✓	*	✓	✓	✓	✓	✓
Christmas Day	December 25	✓	✓	✓	✓	✓	✓	✓	✓	✓	✓	✓	✓	✓
Boxing Day	December 26	*	*	*	*	✓	*	*	*	*	*	*	*	*

Key

Holiday ✓

Possible Holiday *
(depends on workplace)

Vocabulary

Read this sentence: The *reforms* cost money, but the changes helped many people.

The activities below help you understand the word *reform*.
Follow the directions in each box.

reform

1

Read the paragraphs below. As you read, try to figure out the meaning of *reform*.

Tommy Douglas fought for *reforms* in the health care system. Now people do not have to pay for basic health care.

• • • • •

The parents read out a list of *reforms*. The reforms included spending more money on training teachers. The reforms also included making the size of classes smaller.

Now choose the correct meaning for reform.

(a) a way to make money

(b) a change to a system that affects many people in some way

(c) a negative change to a system

2

Read the examples below. Choose two examples that describe reform.

(a) In the past, prisons just punished people. Now prisons help inmates work toward a better life. Prisons provide classes and training for jobs.

(b) The city built a stadium. A few business people made a lot of money.

(c) The voting laws changed. Now people in rural areas have a stronger voice.

Look at your two choices above. Explain why your choices are examples of reform.

Word Attack 1: Predict the Word

Finish the sentences in the paragraph.
You can use any words that make sense.

Everyone loves a holiday. Not all

_____ get the same holidays.

For example, workers in Ontario get Boxing Day

off. But workers in other _____ may not. We

can all enjoy a long _____ when a holiday

falls on Monday or Friday. A day off gives people time to

_____ .

> What do you do if you can't read a word?
>
> Active readers think of a word that makes sense.

Word Attack 2: Letter Patterns

Read the sentences.
Circle two words for each letter pattern.

ing

1. Tommy saw a workers' strike one spring.
2. The strike was one thing that shaped Tommy's life.

eat

3. Tommy saw police beat up and shoot workers.
4. Did the workers want to cheat their bosses?

ack

5. Tommy grew up on the wrong side of the tracks.
6. He went back to school at the age of 20.

> Active readers look for letter patterns. A letter pattern looks and sounds the same. Say these words:
>
> **sound   round   found**
>
> These words all have the same letter pattern.

Word Attack 3: Divide and Conquer

Read each sentence.
Circle the words that have a suffix.
The first one is an example.

1. Tommy was the (leader) of the CCF.

2. The CCF made many new laws.

3. Workers wanted better working conditions.

4. The hours of work per week went down.

5. Workers got two weeks of vacation.

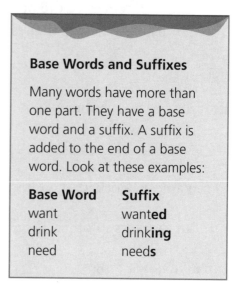

Base Words and Suffixes

Many words have more than one part. They have a base word and a suffix. A suffix is added to the end of a base word. Look at these examples:

Base Word	Suffix
want	want**ed**
drink	drink**ing**
need	need**s**

Read the paragraph.
Add suffixes to complete the words.
The first one is an example.

Tommy watch _ed_ a strike in Winnipeg.

He saw police beat up work____. Tommy

was 14 year____ old. Later, Tommy went into

politic____. He want____ to help people.

On strike in Winnipeg.

Read each sentence.
Find and divide the compound word.

1. Tommy was a newspaper boy.

2. He fought for a shorter workweek.

3. Tommy's grandson was in the TV show *24*.

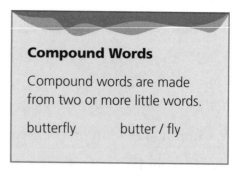

Compound Words

Compound words are made from two or more little words.

butterfly   butter / fly

HISTORY

ANSWER KEY

In some cases, the answer key contains only a few of the possible responses for questions. There are other acceptable responses for these questions.

People

Unit 1: Terry Fox

Check the Facts: 1. Possible responses: Terry got bone cancer. Terry lost his leg to bone cancer. Terry saw many patients die from cancer. Terry believed more cancer research would give patients hope. Terry read a story about a man with one leg who ran a marathon. **2.** b **Discussion: 1.** Student responses will vary. **2.** Student responses will vary. **3.** Student responses will vary.

Mini-Lesson: (p. 5) Possible responses: **Top Chart: 1. Inference:** I think it was the boy's birthday. **Why:** I know that people put candles on birthday cakes. **2. Inference:** I think the vending machine was broken. **Why:** I know that people bang on vending machines if they don't get their change or the item they paid for. **Bottom Chart: 1. Inference:** I think Terry was strong. **Why:** I know that he kept running even when he was in pain or feeling dizzy. **2. Inference:** I think Terry was an important person in Canada. **Why:** I know that only important people's pictures are put on money.

Literacy Practice: 1. Canada **2.** 5 **3.** The city is the capital of a province. **4.** because Ottawa is the capital city of Canada **5.** west **6.** b **7.** Student responses will vary.

Vocabulary: Box 1: 1. b **2.** a **3.** Possible responses: He changed society by making people more aware of how important cancer research is. He inspired people to donate money to cancer research. People with cancer have more hope now. **Box 2: 1.** b **2.** Student responses will vary.

Predict the Word: places; countries; cities; towns / kilometres / directions / map

Letter Patterns: 1. grew **2.** news **3.** shocking **4.** rocky **5.** near **6.** hear

Divide and Conquer: 2. trained; years **3.** cheered **4.** watched; storms **5.** poured **Paragraph:** shocking / news / turned / believed / started **Compound Words: 1.** New/found/land **2.** down/town **3.** out/side

Unit 2: Viola Desmond

Check the Facts: 1. A newspaper for black people picked up Viola's story. Then more newspapers started reporting her case, so lots of people heard about it. **2.** b **Discussion: 1.** Possible responses: More people became aware of racism, so there was more pressure on the government to make changes. People's attitudes toward racism have changed, so the government's attitude needs to change, too. The black community never stopped putting pressure on the government. The government did not want to look bad. **2.** Student responses will vary. **3.** Student responses will vary.

Mini-Lesson: (p. 14) Possible responses: **1. Inference:** I think the police did not respect Viola. **Why:** I know that the police should not treat people roughly. **2. Inference:** I think Viola did not get a fair trial. **Why:** I know that trials usually take a long time. **(p. 15)** Possible responses: **Paragraph 1.** I think Viola was a strong, independent person. Viola knew what she wanted and went after it. Viola did not give up. **Paragraph 2:** I think Viola influenced Wanda. I think Wanda respected Viola.

Literacy Practice: (p. 16) 1. b **2a.** No. The boss expects Dan to sit in a child's rocking chair. **2b.** Possible responses: The boss is treating Dan like a child. The boss is treating Dan as though Dan were stupid. The boss is not treating Dan with respect. **3a.** Possible responses: angry, insulted, sad, helpless **3b.** Student responses will vary. **4.** b

Vocabulary: Box 1: 1. a, c **2.** black people were separated from society because of race. **Box 2:** c Jewish people were separated from society because of their religion.

Predict the Word: laugh; smile; think / important; many; political; eduational / opinions; ideas; feelings / happy; angry; thoughtful; sad

Letter Patterns: 1. place **2.** races **3.** night **4.** fight **5.** built **6.** guilty

Divide and Conquer: 2. wanted **3.** pulled **4.** spending **5.** appeals **Paragraph:** owners / places / schools / laws / helped **Compound Words: 1.** news/papers **2.** every/one **3.** no/thing

Relationships

Unit 3: Personal Harassment

Check the Facts: 1. They take sick days to avoid the harasser. They ignore what is going on. They talk to the harasser. They phone the CHRC. **2.** a **Discussion: 1a.** No. A boss has a right to scold you for being late. (But he should do it in an adult way.) **1b.** Yes. The boss is making you feel small. He is embarrassing you. He makes you feel bad. **1c.** No. The name-calling happened only once. Everyone loses their temper once in awhile. **2.** Student responses will vary. **3.** Student responses will vary.

Mini-Lesson: (p. 24) Supporting details: 1. He called Sara names. **2.** He hid Sara's tools.
(p. 25) Paragraph 1: Main idea: c **Supporting details: 1.** ignore what is going on **2.** ask the harasser to stop **Paragraph 2: Main idea:** b **Supporting details: 1.** dates of the harassment **2.** who was there **3.** what was said or done

THE ACTIVE READER

Literacy Practice: (p. 26) 1. Possible responses: types of job, location, duties, required qualifications **2a.** per hour **2b.** hours per week **2c.** experience **2d.** required **2e.** full-time **2f.** part-time **(p. 27)** Student responses will vary.

Vocabulary: Box 1: 1. She makes Rex do all the dirty jobs and paperwork. **2.** She does not have to the dirty jobs or any paperwork. She feels powerful and in control. **3.** He does not complain because he is new to the job. He is new to the job and does not realize he is being exploited. He needs the work. He is afraid of losing the job if he complains. **Box 2: 1a.** He is getting more work done for less money. He will look good in the eyes of his boss. He feels powerful. **1b.** She is working illegally, so she cannot complain to anyone. **2a.** Rick is exploiting Leo. **2b.** Rick is getting free haircuts and free hair products. **2c.** Rick is Leo's friend, and Leo does not want to hurt their friendship.

Predict the Word: good; efficient; common / newspapers / hours; shifts; location; duties; requirements / application; resume

Letter Patterns: 1. boss **2.** loss **3.** picks **4.** sick **5.** should **6.** could

Divide and Conquer: 1. jokes **2.** unwanted; touching **3.** includes; repeated **4.** treats; workers; children **5.** Harassment; makes **Paragraph:** going / turning / feels / harasser **Compound Words: 1.** work/place **2.** some/one **3.** some/thing

Unit 4: Getting Along

Check the Facts: 1a. Possible responses: change the way we listen, change the subject, say nothing **1b.** change the direction of the conversation **1c.** avoid arguing **2.** a **Discussion:** Possible responses: **1a.** Co-workers might start to complain more. They might do less work. They might start to dislike their jobs. Some co-workers might feel pressure to go along with the complaining. **1b.** The workplace will be less pleasant. Morale might go down. There might be less trust between the workers and the company. **2.** Student responses will vary. **3.** Student responses will vary.

Mini-Lesson: Paragraph 1: Main idea: b **Supporting details: 1.** speak well of the person **2.** change the subject **3.** say you do not want to talk about other people **Paragraph 2: Main idea:** c **Supporting details: 1.** Asking questions shows we want to hear more. **2.** We need to stop asking questions. **Paragraph 3: Main idea:** b **Supporting details: 1.** even people we like act in unwanted ways **2.** we cannot change co-workers **3.** it takes careful thinking and skill

Literacy Practice: Student responses will vary.

Vocabulary: Box 1: c **Box 2:** b

Predict the Word: decisions; friends / people; co-workers / fun; easy; enjoyable; hard

Letter Patterns: 1. more **2.** chore **3.** need **4.** feed **5.** wrong **6.** strong

Divide and Conquer: 1. things **2.** being; fired **3.** pointing; fingers; co-workers **4.** fixing **5.** Talking; helps **Paragraph:** unwanted / complaining / gossiping / co-workers / times / takes / thinking **Compound Words: 1.** can/not **2.** some/one **3.** every/thing

Health and Safety

Unit 5: Food Poisoning

Check the Facts: 1. Do not thaw food at room temperature. Keep vegetables and milk products away from raw meat, poultry, and fish. Note cooking times and temperatures. **2.** b **Discussion: 1.** You should keep raw meat away from vegetables. Maya uses the same tongs to handle raw hamburger and serve salad. Bacteria on the hamburger could get on the salad. The bacteria on the hamburger will die with cooking, but the bacteria on the salad will live. **2.** Student responses will vary. **3.** Student responses will vary.

Mini-Lesson: (p. 44) 1. F/O **2.** O/F **3.** F/O **4.** O/F **1.** F **2.** F **3.** O **4.** F **5.** O
(p. 45) Paragraph 1: Everybody thinks all bacteria are bad. **Paragraph 2:** Bacteria are the most interesting form of life in the world.

Literacy Practice: 1. Possible unclear parts: thick slices / pieces / thin strips / to taste / squares **2.** Possible unclear parts: Blend well / medium-high heat / until chicken meat is white / until vegetables are tender-crisp

Vocabulary: Box 1: b **Box 2:** a

Predict the Word: vegetables; pasta; poultry / ingredients; items / cook; prepare; serve / stir; chop; cut; pour; blend

Letter Patterns: 1. smell **2.** tell **3.** cook **4.** Look **5.** Thaw **6.** raw

Divide and Conquer: 1. spots **2.** cramps **3.** started; throwing **4.** poisoning **5.** learned **Paragraph:** cooking / times / temperatures / temperatures / vegetables / products **Compound Words: 1.** left/over **2.** with/in **3.** Lunch/time

Unit 6: Skin Cancer

Check the Facts: 1. UVB rays are the main cause of skin cancer. They heat the skin. They can pass through clothing. They are strongest between 10 a.m. and 4 p.m. They can pass through clouds. They can bounce off sand, water, snow, and concrete. **2.** a **Discussion: 1.** Yes. UVB rays pass through clouds even in the winter. They bounce off the snow. **2.** Student responses will vary. **3.** Student responses will vary.

Mini-Lesson: (p. 54) 1. O/F **2.** F/O **3.** O/F **4.** O/F **1.** F **2.** O **3.** F **4.** O **5.** F
(p. 55) Paragraph 1: I believe people at risk will get skin cancer no matter what they do.
Paragraph 2: Most parents do not protect their children from the sun.

Literacy Practice: 1. Student responses will vary. **2.** a c d **3a.** Possible response: Ask a pharmacist. **3b.** Student responses will vary. **3c.** Possible responses: to keep the skin soft, to make the sunscreen smell nice, to make the sunscreen more natural or healthy **4.** No. The sunscreen expires in 2014.

Vocabulary: Box 1: Student responses will vary. **Box 2: 1.** c **2.** a **3.** b

Predict the Word: ingredients; chemicals / directions; instructions; warnings / children; kids / harmful; dangerous; poisonous

Letter Patterns: 1. small **2.** called **3.** patch **4.** catch **5.** check **6.** neck

Divide and Conquer: 2. months **3.** changes **4.** looks **5.** crusty; patches **Paragraph:** days / trees / rays / clouds / rays **Compound Words: 1.** sun/screen **2.** sun/burn **3.** sun/glasses

Environment

Unit 7: Deepwater

Check the Facts: 1a. The oil spill killed turtles, seabirds, and dolphins. It washed into marshes and wetlands. It washed onto beaches. It reduced the number of fish, shrimp, oysters, and crabs. **1b.** Tourist towns lost money. People lost their jobs. **2.** a **Discussion: 1.** Possible responses: Nobody wanted to take the blame because the oil spill was so big. The oil spill was going to be very expensive to clean up. Companies did not want to lose business. The government did not want to look bad. It is easier to blame someone else than take responsibility. **2.** Student responses will vary. **3.** Student responses will vary.

Mini-Lesson: (p. 65) Idea Map 2: Effect: Tourist towns lost money and jobs. **Effect:** Fishing areas were shut down.

Literacy Practice: 1. How Canadians Use Energy in Homes (2007) **2a.** 4% **2b.** 13% **3a.** 81% **3b.** by reading the text, or by adding up the percentages for heating homes and heating water **4.** Possible responses: Canada has short summers, so people need to air condition their homes only a few months of the year. A lot of people do not have air conditioning. **5.** Student responses will vary.

Vocabulary: Box 1: Student responses will vary. **Box 2: 1.** b **2.** c **3.** a

Predict the Word: oil; coal; wood / winter / homes; houses; apartments; water / stoves; toasters; blenders; microwaves

Letter Patterns: 1. main **2.** stain **3.** reached **4.** beaches **5.** towns **6.** down

Divide and Conquer: 1. hundreds; turtles **2.** killed; seabirds; dolphins **3.** washed; marshes; wetlands **4.** fishing; areas **5.** affected; oysters; crabs **Paragraph:** boats / miles / floating / booms / booms / helped / spreading / boats / sucked / chemicals **Compound Words: 1.** Sea/water **2.** Deep/water **3.** wet/lands

Unit 8: The Cleanup

Check the Facts: 1. People sent in hair and fur to make hair booms. People became coast watchers. **2.** b **Discussion: 1.** Possible responses: people who are interested in the environment, retired people (because they have free time), people who live near a beach **2.** Student responses will vary. **3.** Student responses will vary.

Mini-Lesson: Paragraph 1: Effect: The turtles were sick and not eating. **Paragraph 2: Effect:** Many turtles got better and gained weight. **Paragraph 3: Effect:** Sea animals and birds suffer and die. **Effect:** Beaches and wetlands turn black with oil. **Effect:** People come together.

Literacy Practice: 1. ABC Utility Company **2.** July **3.** $86.50 **4.** $46.50 **5.** a **6.** You need to add the balance from the last bill and the penalty fee to the new charges. **7.** b **8.** b **9a.** (555) 555-2222 **9b.** 55631411-A

Vocabulary: Box 1: a **Box 2: 1.** 2, 3, 6 **2.** Student responses will vary.

Predict the Word: month / power; electricity; gas / address; account; number; charges; balance / number

Letter Patterns: 1. floats **2.** boats **3.** spills **4.** kill **5.** hope **6.** cope

Divide and Conquer: 2. called **3.** watchers; walked **4.** walked; beaches **5.** looked; animals; covered **Paragraph:** pictures / videos / watchers / phoned / Disasters / finding / brings **Compound Words: 1.** clean/up **2.** hot/line **3.** hair/cut

History

Unit 9: Workers' Rights

Check the Facts: 1. business owners, local politicians, members of the Citizens' Committee of 1000, the federal government, the special police, the Army, the Mounted Police **2.** b **Discussion: 1.** Possible responses: If the strikers were successful, the government would have to pay its workers more. The government would have to spend money on improving working conditions. The strike could spread across the country. **2.** Student responses will vary. **3.** Student responses will vary.

Mini-Lesson: (p.84) 1. b **2a.** May 15 **2b.** June 26 **2c.** 6 **3.** b **(p.85) 1.** The X should be placed on the midway marker between the years 1865 and 1875. **2.** a **3a.** 1884 **3b.** ii **4.** ii

Literacy Practice: 1. The Pet Shop Inc. **2.** November 14 **3.** b **4.** overtime **5.** income tax **6.** $672.55 **7.** b **8.** c **9.** b

Vocabulary: Box 1: a **Box 2:** a

Predict the Word: money / weeks / boss; company; workplace

Letter Patterns: 1. like **2.** strike **3.** mail **4.** jail **5.** streets **6.** meet

Divide and Conquer: 1. workers **2.** members; unions **3.** unions; joined **4.** unions; asked **5.** leaders; ended **Paragraph:** workers / filled / streets / chased / workers / streets / guns / killed **Compound Words: 1.** down/town **2.** work/day **3.** over/time

Unit 10: Father of Medicare

Check the Facts: 1. Tommy's family was poor, so Tommy learned what it was like to grow up poor. A doctor helped Tommy by working on his leg for free, and Tommy went on to fight for medicare. Tommy saw a brutal strike, and he went on to fight for better working conditions. **2.** a **Discussion: 1.** Possible responses: Tommy chose jobs that helped people. Tommy felt he could do more for people as a politician. **2.** Student responses will vary. **3.** Student responses will vary.

Mini-Lesson: (p.94) 1. The X should be placed on the midway marker between the years 1900 and 1920. **2.** 1930 **3a.** 1934 **3b.** 1979 **3c.** 45 **(p.95) 1.** 1914 **2a.** 1965 **2b.** 45 **3.** Student responses will vary.

Literacy Practice: 1. Holidays in Canada **2a.** SK **2b.** QC **2c.** YT **3.** November 11 **4a.** 2 **4b.** * **5.** New Year's Day; Canada Day; Labour Day; Christmas Day **6a.** T **6b.** F **6c.** T **7.** Student responses will vary.

Vocabulary: Box 1: b **Box 2:** a,c

Predict the Word: people; workers / provinces; places; areas / weekend / relax; rest; catch up

Letter Patterns: 1. spring **2.** thing **3.** beat **4.** cheat **5.** tracks **6.** back

Divide and Conquer: 2. laws **3.** workers; wanted; working; conditions **4.** hours **5.** workers; weeks **Paragraph:** workers / years / politics / wanted **Compound Words: 1.** news/paper **2.** work/week **3.** grand/son